# CONTEMPORARY
# PICTORIAL QUILTS

WENDY LAVITT

**F**OR **M**EL, **K**ATHY, **J**OHN AND **M**EREDITH

97 96 95 94 93   10 9 8 7 6 5 4 3 2 1

This is a Peregrine Smith Book, published by
Gibbs Smith, Publisher
P.O. Box 667
Layton, Utah  84041


Cover and interior design by Connie Witt-Christensen
Heather Bennett, Editor
Lynda Sessions Sorenson, Editor
Dawn Valentine, Editorial Assistant


Printed in Hong Kong by South Sea International Press


Library of Congress Cataloging-in-Publication Data

Lavitt, Wendy
        Pictorial quilts/Wendy Lavitt
                p.        cm.
        ISBN o-87905-557-x
        1. Quilts—United States—Themes, motives. 2.Quilts—
United States—History—20th century—Themes, motives.
I.Title.
NK9112.L38    1993
746.3973—dc20

                                                92-42975
                                                     CIP

# CONTENTS

In *Contemporary Pictorial Quilts*, thread and cloth join brush and canvas as recognized tools of the art world. The quiltmakers—most but not all of them women—seek to satisfy their own creativity without sacrificing communication. They strive to translate personal experiences into universally affecting images. Some of the quilts featured in this book have been the product of a coping mechanism, a way to work out emotional problems and deal with events beyond the control of the artists. They are as infused with drama as they are with color. Other quilts are oases of serenity, replete with golden landscapes and dreamlike idylls that blur the hard edges of reality. Quilts portraying life in the fast lane beat with the syncopated rhythm of city streets, subways, and markets. All of the quilts reflect the varied life experiences of the quilters and their unique perceptions of the contemporary scene. Moving into the twenty-first century is a heady, but precipitous journey; these quilts radiate the excitement of our times. They challenge us to connect with the joys, fears, hopes, and disappointments of today's pictorial quilters. On another level, the quilts demand to be appreciated as examples of superb technical skill and innovative design.

Since most contemporary pictorial quilters are no longer content with the concept of a quilt as a utilitarian object, they insist their quilts are not dependent on function. By experimenting with new techniques involving asymmetrical contours, three-dimensional images, and unusual collages of materials, many pictorial quilters are extending the boundaries of their art. They offer new definitions of the nature of a quilt. They revel in the sensuality of fabric, believing the process of quilting gives them an opportunity to go beyond the look-but-don't-touch confines of painting. Nevertheless, pictorial quilt artists are the first to admit their debt to such major

schools of painting as impressionism, cubism, and realism. Many pictorial quilters have formal training in art which holds them to rigorous standards in the use of form, space, and movement. Other makers, self-taught or members of quilting guilds and classes, have equally exacting yardsticks by which they measure their art. The result is a stunning body of work encompassing both traditional and groundbreaking pictorial images.

Quilts have been called metaphors in art, utilizing a language readily understood by the viewer. The language of quilts is enhanced by color, which brings to life figures and forms. Almost all pictorial quilters are colorists who are as passionate about tone and hue as they are about texture. Increasing numbers of pictorial quilters are dyeing their own cloth to achieve the exact gradation of color they require. As exacting as painters mixing pigments on a palette, these quilters manipulate their raw material by dyeing, staining, painting, and coloring with crayons or pencils. Artists enjoy the search for a perfect fabric, haunting remnant stores, fabric outlets, and thrift shops. They speak of the thrill of finding a piece of fabric that is the missing jigsaw piece in a composition. Occasionally an accidental find is the inspiration for a new quilt.

The subjects pictorial quilters choose are infinite, reflecting facets of the imagination. Perusing the numerous quilting magazines on the market today and attending exhibitions and quilt conventions, you can spot the latest trends. Most of the contemporary quilts I viewed fit into the chapters that make up this book. While some of the subjects chosen by contemporary pictorial quilters would undoubtedly appeal to their predecessors, others would puzzle and shock them. Quilts recounting memories of childhood, celebrations of holidays, and rural scenes often follow more traditional models; while quilts inspired by the women's movement and the current political climate express unsettling concerns in more innovative ways. Still, they owe a debt to the long tradition of social-reform quilts that confronted such nineteenth-century ills as alcoholism and the horrors of the Civil War.

On a personal level, pictorial quilters today exhibit an eagerness to explore subjects that once were veiled in secrecy. Part of the process is the desire to share innermost feelings with various networks, including the quilter's family, art critics, gallery patrons, and fellow artists. Increasing numbers of quilters are reaching out to a larger audience, even when it means exposing painful episodes in their lives. A celebrated example, *The Divorce Quilt*, by Katherine Brainard (p.120) appeared in *People* magazine in May of 1991, defining the agony of the end of Brainard's ten-year marriage. Calling it "cathartic—a healing process," Brainard didn't hesitate to share her anger with the world, using the quilt as therapy to overcome feelings of bitterness and sadness. In a sense, *The Divorce Quilt* can be called a family document, a modern version of a traditional type of pictorial quilt. Quilts validating domestic history focus on rites of passage such as birth, courtship, graduation, marriage, and death. Many of these pictorial quilts have been made as family gifts that are handed down from generation to generation. Such modern legacies are unique interpretations of the world, destined to become treasured heirlooms.

As I researched this book, meeting and speaking with artists in over twenty-five states, I was impressed with the level of commitment demonstrated by both artists who have the advantage of working full time in well-equipped studios and those who work at home, often on a kitchen table, snatching blocks of time from busy schedules. Some quilts which had been promised for this volume were late getting finished due to the vicissitudes of life, but finished they were—even if it meant staying up nights and putting other priorities on hold. As the artists' statements came in, I found myself admiring the writing skills of an articulate group of men and women. While some preferred to let their work speak for itself, many more chose to expound in great detail on the meaning of their quilts and the techniques they employed. It was a pleasure and an honor to be included for a short time in the lives of such a talented and creative group.

Finally, one of the most compelling reasons for collecting quilt books is the inspiration they provide. A faraway look glazes the eyes of artists as they speak of the hours spent poring over these books, comparing their work to the work of their peers, admiring the "stars," and, of course, dreaming of new quilts. While some of us who enjoy these books have never made a quilt, we can always think of 'someday.' It is my fondest hope that the quilts in the following chapters will unleash the passion to create pictorial quilts that will define the first decade of the next century.

**BALTIMORE ALBUM QUILT**

Mary Evans (Workshop); 1847–1850; 104 1/4 x 103 1/4 inches; quilted fabrics; courtesy of Hirschl and Adler, New York, New York

# **N**INETEENTH AND **T**WENTIETH **C**ENTURIES

**A**merica's first pictorial quilts were made as early as the eighteenth century. Indian chintz bedspreads, decorated with hand-painted floral designs and Tree of Life motifs, are regarded as the forerunners of today's pictorial quilts. A popular variation in the late eighteenth and early nineteenth centuries, the *Broderie Perse* bedcover, was assembled from a variety of chintz motifs stitched to the background fabric. Flowers, foliage, exotic birds, butterflies, urns, and floral baskets graced these counterpanes in appliqué form. Quilters could look to a pictorial legacy from England where at least one early quilt adorned with dozens of figures, animals, and objects surrounded by a chintz border has been preserved. It is pictured in the December 14, 1935 edition of *Country Life*.

In the mid-nineteenth century, a new fad appeared: the album quilt. Constructed of appliqué blocks, the album quilt was made by women as a form of remembrance for special occasions. The elaborate, highly styled Baltimore album quilt with brilliantly colored appliqués sewn on a white ground incorporated excit-ing pictorial images. Innovative subjects, including modes of transportation, buildings, genre scenes and every conceivable example of flora and fauna were depicted in less formal album quilts, samplers, and hooked rugs. Many women completed these projects under less than ideal circumstances. Poignant accounts of quilts created in sod houses, log cabins, and dugouts abound in pioneer histories.

> Mama's best quilts were her dugout quilts because that was when she really needed something pretty. She made a Butterfly and a Dresden Plate and a Flower Basket during those two years in the dugout.... She made the Basket for Papa. She started the Butterfly in that first dust storm all alone.... The Butterfly was free and fragile. It was the prettiest thing she could think of. She knew I was coming along and the Butterfly was for me."[1]

Women from inland villages and farms executed less sophisticated quilts than those made in the cities where shops were stocked with a variety of fabrics and new designs originated. Conversely, the isolation of the rural quilter sometimes led to innovative pictorial quilts that relied more upon the quilter's imagination and less upon convention. Women everywhere found solace in appliqué quilts celebrating births and weddings or commemorating deaths. Textile works exploring life and death were almost always connected to spiritual themes. Religious scenes and familiar biblical stories, such as the Garden of Eden and Noah's

Ark, form an important part of pictorial quilt history in the nineteenth century.

The motifs in decorative arts are rooted in the lexicon of nineteenth century quilts. It has been noted that "nearly every non-geometric design found on a Baltimore Album quilt can also be found as the central motif on a piece of Staffordshire."[2] Women also looked for inspiration in the popular Jacquard coverlets featuring multi-colored woven designs of birds, animals, buildings, floral designs, and patriotic symbols. Regional influences, especially the Pennsylvania German decorative arts, are seen in pictorial quilts containing tulips, angels, hearts, and the ubiquitous *distelfink*. A man and a woman, drawn facing each other on Pennsylvania German baptismal certificates, appear in many versions of Baltimore album quilts and fold quilts of the nineteenth century. Since relatively few women were encouraged to write or paint, many expressed their thoughts with the needle, choosing their images from an array of decorative pictorial elements. Telling stories through their quilts represented an important creative outlet for such women.

One of the landmarks in nineteenth-century quilting was the Centennial Exposition of 1876. While rural women had always entered quilts in county fairs, they had never encountered the excitement of the Centennial Exposition, which marked a new awareness and appreciation of the art of quilting. While few entries could be called pictorial by today's standards, the popular silk and velvet crazy quilts featured many pictorial elements. The crazy quilt challenged the accepted definition of a quilt with its innovative techniques of ornamentation. Beads, metallic thread, painting on silk and elaborate trims had never been seen on quilts before. Today artists routinely incorporate a variety of objects in their pictorial quilts, sometimes looking back to the crazy quilt for inspiration. Quilt historians also note that for the first time the quilt migrated from the bedroom to the parlor. Thrown over a chair or piano for a decorative accent, the crazy quilt foretold the wall quilt of the twentieth century.

In 1905 the *Ladies Home Journal* commissioned five well-known artists (including Maxfield Parrish) to design appliqué pictorials for their readers. Although these patterns—which featured circus and animal scenes—were suited for the nursery, they were also strikingly decorative and served to introduce the concept of pictorial quilts to a large audience. In the early twentieth century the wide dissemination of quilt patterns in magazines and newspapers across the country exposed new styles and ideas to quilters in even the most isolated areas. No longer solely dependent on handed-down patterns, they were encouraged to experiment.

It wasn't until the Sears National Quilt Contest in 1933, however, that pictorial quilts received national attention. More than 24,000 quilters vied for top prizes totaling $7500. A bonus of $200 was offered to the grand prizewinner whose design featured the theme of the fair, "A Century of Progress." For the first time a national contest *advertised* for pictorial quilts. The quilts in this category heralded advances in transportation and industry while they celebrated historical events. Although these quilts received attention in the media, none made it to the winners' circle—even at the regional finals. The judges' apparent bias for traditional (that is, non-representational) patterns angered the makers of those Century-of-Progress quilts being displayed at the fair. Still, thousands came to see the pictorial quilts. Who knows how many quilters went away with the idea that they could make one themselves?

The ensuing years saw a decline in quilting. The war years found more women in the factories, while those who had the time for quilting seemed to prefer manufactured goods. The attitude that quilting was "old-fashioned" and that "store-bought" was better prevailed through the 1950s and 1960s. It wasn't until the 1970s during the "craft" revival that quilting was looked upon anew, and that the "art quilt" or "wall-quilt" emerged from obscurity to prominence. By the 1990s the rage for pictorial quilts had become a national phenomenon.

1. *The Quilters: Women and Domestic Art.* Patricia Cooper and Norma Bradley Buferd: Anchor Press (1978), p. 24.

2. *Baltimore Album Quilts.* Dena S. Katzenberg: The Baltimore Museum of Art (1980), p. 45.

**UNTITLED**
Elizabeth B. Jones (Caldwell County, Kentucky); 1881; no measurements given; courtesy of the Ames Gallery of Folk Art, Berkeley, California

**"CRAZY QUILT"**
Katherine Knauer (New York, New York); 1988; 64 x 64 inches; quilted fabrics; photo by Karen Bell

**NANTUCKET QUILT**
1847–1850; 70 x 83 inches; courtesy of Laura Fisher Antiques, New York, New York

**A CURIOSITY BEDSPREAD**

Mrs. Avery Burton (Duck Hill, Mississippi); 1935; 73 x 75 inches; cotton appliqué; courtesy of Shelley Zegart, Louisville, Kentucky

## NIGHTFALL

Lura Schwarz Smith (Coarsegold, California); 1992; 38 x 48 inches; cottons, silks, synthetics, and panne velvet

In this wall piece I worked with a combination of piecing and appliqué techniques. Many types of fabrics were used: sheers, metallics, velvets and cottons. I enjoy incorporating non-traditional fabrics into wall hangings and the richness of texture this can achieve.

The image is one that has long interested me, and it is the second version of the theme. *Nightfall* is a combination of a dream and an illustration I once saw of a child rolled into a star-sprinkled blanket that became the night. I love working with my dream images, and they form the basis for much of the imagery in my fabric work.

# INNER FEELINGS

The journeys of pictorial quilts from random shapes to meaningful forms reflect the artists' individual struggles and growth. Through fabric they are challenged to convey visually their deepest feelings and private histories. Each artist employs personal techniques and symbols to express these feelings and many consider their work a form of meditation.

In creating quilts that deal with highly charged subjects, artists often note that the experience of translating feelings has led them to explore new styles. Darcy Homes's *He was Dying* changed her style, she says, "forever," resulting in a new body of work characterized by its darkly evocative elements. She claims that subsequent quilts are more richly embellished and deeply textured than previous pieces. By experiencing an artistic epiphany she was able to explore personal visions through the juxtaposition of fabrics. Quilts of this genre are sometimes ambiguous, employing symbols the viewer might or might not understand. To fully appreciate Cherry Partee's quilts the viewer must be acquainted with various symbols of Western culture and religion. Even the

sophisticated might wonder about Partee's intent. This suits Partee just fine. She hopes that "it is not possible to completely explicate *Consuming the White Rose*—it should mean something different to each person." Visions, dreams and altered states float upon memories in very private worlds. Roxana Bartlett in her statement concerning *The Light of Other Days* speaks of moments "more clearly felt than understood." Lura Schwarz-Smith's *Nightfall* was partly inspired by a dream that formed the focal point for its evocative images.

One of the saddest quilts in this section, Anne Warren's *Seeds of Destruction*, recalls the famous AIDS quilt in which each of the 15,840 panels represents someone who died of AIDS. Warren's novel approach depicts virus particles hovering over a vulnerable blood cell at the onset of the disease. Although at first glance the molecules appear to be colorful assemblages, their chilling message is as powerful a statement as any presented in this chapter.

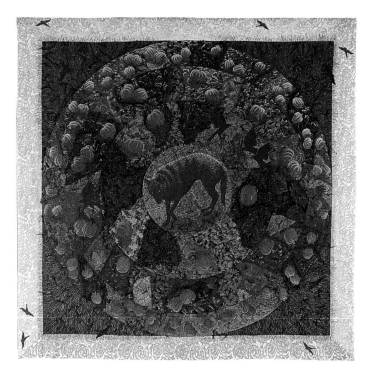

### THE LIGHT OF OTHER DAYS

Roxana Bartlett (Boulder, Colorado); 1991; 68 1/2 x 68 1/2 inches; assorted fabrics, procion dye, acrylic paint, and wool yarn; photo by Ken Sanville

The light at a particular time of day can resonate within us. In the sensations of that moment our essential-self merges with this expression of the physical world. All our joys and all our sorrows come rushing upon us, and as in a dream or the memories of long ago, the moment is more clearly felt than understood.

The fabrics in this quilt are over-dyed, cut, and pieced together by hand and machine. The images were then painted with acrylics or appliquéd. The quilt was tied with wool yarn.

### HE WAS DYING

Darcy Holmes (Madison, Wisconsin); 1988; 72 x 48 inches; wool, velvet, silk, yarn, and paint

Tom lay in the hospital waiting for a new heart. I had been told that if Tom did not receive a heart for transplant he would in all probability die. One night I woke up hearing death dogs howling. I knew there was nothing in the whole world that I could do but wait—either for death or for Tom's new heart. He received a new heart. One year later he left me.

I believe that *He Was Dying* changed my style forever. I use a wider variety of textures. I embellish in deeper layers. My work is darker—deeply emotional, personal. People always ask me for more details. They want to hear the story, the whole story. I've been asked how I can use fabrics that are so enticing, so beautiful that they create feelings. Obviously this is exactly what I want to do. I believe that *He Was Dying* is my masterpiece.

**REFUGE OF SELF**

Francelise Dawkins (Glens Falls, New York); 1991; 17 1/2 x 15 inches; silk, velvet and African cotton prints

In the cold month of February 1992 in upstate New York I made this piece after visiting a greenhouse. The faces of three women and a child prodigy emerge out of tropical plants. Equally alive are plants and expressive looks which can travel deep in our subconscious. I wanted to symbolize the child within and the three women inside of me: seductive, contemplative or paradoxical. The one in the middle resembles my French Caribbean grandmother as she appeared to me in a dream long ago, planting in me the seed of patience. I found the title of the piece after reading the book *The Teachings of the Compassionate Buddha*, from which I understood that in the heart of our nature the Self is always safe.

I call my works "silkollages" to convey the idea that silk enters into the composition of my collages. To build a silkollage I use metallic, wool or cotton fabrics and threads, together with a variety of silks from Thailand, India, or Japan. A silkollage is made up of four layers of material—quilted, appliquéd, embroidered or painted on. My sense of colors is influenced by my Caribbean mother, a costume designer whose work trained my eye to accept bold luminosity.

**CONSUMING THE WHITE ROSE**

Cherry Partee (Edmonds, Washington); 1991; 90 x 100 inches; cotton damask, Neopaque fabric paint, glass beads; photo by Grover Partee

**O**ne of the characteristics of the mature human being is responsibility. In this work I considered a problem that all people face, that is, the problem of self-knowledge, self-construction, and what is entailed in creating the continually redefined self.

*Consuming the White Rose* may be read from left to right as one would read English text. The human figure may be considered to be two people or aspects of one person. The construction of the wall creates an ambiguous spatial perspective with the standing figure occupying the edge of a niche of infinitely receding space which is obviously too deep to be accommodated by the thin broken wall above the seated figure. To survive, people tend to create in their minds stable, predictable structures even though bits of knowledge continually force human beings to break down and reconstruct these structures. In Western culture the crow and knowledge are closely associated with sin and death. From "the knowledge of good and evil" in the Garden of Eden to contemporary book burnings and censorship battles, we are exhorted to close our eyes to evil. The white rose of innocence whispers seductively in our ear, "If you do not know, how can you be guilty?" Close your eyes and deny the flush of life, close your eyes and be a child always. Knowledge brings power. Power brings growth and joy and life. Life brings change and pain. Better always to turn away. Better to close your eyes and sleep the sleep of the spiritually dead.

I hope that it is not possible to completely describe this piece. I hope it means something different to each viewer.

## DOORS OF OUR LIVES

Natasha Kempers-Cullen (Bowdoinham, Maine); 1991; 36 x 24 inches; hand-painted on cottons, glass beads

I was challenged earlier this year to do some small work. I think these door pieces are successful because their smallness draws the viewer in closer and each panel is a rich tapestry of many details. It is easy to imagine each image on a grander scale. As I designed each piece, I was thinking about various aspects of myself and my life. The titles reflect these thoughts: *Party Time, Home Sweet Home, You Gotta Have Art, Alternative Medicine, Do Not Disturb,* and *Honeymoon Sweet.*

**SEPARATE LIVES**

Janice Anthony (Brooks, Maine); 1987; 31 x 40 inches; cotton

*Separate Lives* was one of a series of painted quilts in which I was concerned with elements of architecture within the landscape. The curved staircases reappeared consistently through the series, developing from my affinity for curved lines and abstract structure. I find the tension between the human order of architecture and the disorder of natural forces fascinating. Combined into the subject of one quilt, these elements began to convey an underlying unease within a lyrical setting. At the same time the sources and colors of light are dispersed differently by man-made and natural structures, creating a challenge for the artist. Fabric itself reflects light in its own way, with a softness and surface relief that is unique.

*Separate Lives* in particular has an autobiographical content, a subtext of communication and possibility. I always see when I finish a piece that I have again painted my own life.

**SEEDS OF DESTRUCTION**

Anne Warren (Jefferson, Ohio); 1991; 58 x 72 inches; cottons, some hand-dyed fabrics by the artist, and rip-stop nylon; photo by David Tuhm

Using imagery taken from electron micrographs of the AIDS virus, the quilt depicts three virus particles hovering above a blood cell. The moment of virus attachment is the true beginning of the infection. Since our dominant metaphor for AIDS is invasion of the self from outside, the viruses look like alien spacecraft about to land on an unsuspecting planet. Images at the four corners of the quilt depict the ways in which the infection can spread: via blood, sex, shared needles, or across the placenta. The euphemistic acronyms around the border of the quilt (HIV, ARC, PWA, etc.) represent the dehumanization that can follow diagnosis. The strident neon colors of the viruses and the border are meant to be the visual equivalent of a warning siren or scream. In contrast, the cool blues and green of the cell represent life.

Both hand and machine techniques were used in the piecing, appliqué, piping and quilting of this work. The area of the cell, made of hand-dyed fabric, is hand-quilted in patterns based on intracellular structures as seen under the microscope.

**DRAGON TEA**

Lura Schwarz Smith (Coarsegold, California); 1990; 24 inches in diameter; cottons, satins, metallic fabrics, Ultrasuede, lace

**T**his piece was made in early 1990 for the "Quilt a Modern Fairy Tale" contest sponsored by Kjeldsen's (now Dansk) Cookie Company of Denmark that was advertised in *Quilter's Newsletter Magazine*. Placing second in the contest, it was shown in Odense, Denmark as a side-line to Quilt Europa in May of 1990. It is one of three winners from the contest to be printed as cookie tin designs in a special edition.

The image is a combination of several elements—some of them inspired by my memories of life in San Francisco for two years as an art student—the cozy evenings in our tiny apartment as the fog rolled in over the Golden Gate Bridge and our fondness for Chinatown and the excellent yet reasonable food obtainable there on our tight student budgets. Somewhere along the way this blended with images from the wonderful little fantasy novel, *Tea with the Black Dragon*, by R. A. Macavoy, set in modern-day San Francisco and involving a man who had once been an Imperial Chinese Dragon. Chinese dragons being not at all the vicious, voracious sort in European mythology, I could well imagine sitting down to a cozy tea with one.

Technically, I chose a variety of fabrics and used markers, dye, fabric paint and pencils to achieve effects.

# FANTASY AND PLEASURES

**E**ach of the quilts in *Fantasy and Pleasures* transmits a dream, a joyful recollection, a scene from a fairy tale, or a pleasurable event that left a lasting impression upon the artist. Nowhere is it more evident that the emotional content of pictorial quilts transcends the limits of spoken language. Artists create these quilts, unlocking their personal dreams, daring to share their private moments. These quilts sing with joy; their gay colors are a testament to the feelings of the artists.

The work in this chapter depends upon visual memories. While Marie Combs recreates the romance of the Casbah from old movies, she also draws upon the hours spent as a child curled up with *The Arabian Nights*. Ann Johnston wanted to capture childhood memories, especially the splendors of the Merry-Go-Round. Margaret Cusack chose a more tangible memory, an actual wedding photograph of long ago, for her evocative quilt. These visual impressions were selected to create a mood of wonder and longing, nowhere more evident than in Marjory Claybrook's *Night Offering*. As the women "collect stars from the night sky," their world draws the viewer into reverie—clearly the intention of its creator.

Often a dream of fantasy depends on a fleeting moment or a chance encounter. *Hang Glider Over Yosemite* by Laura Lee Fritz resulted from her good fortune of just happening to drive by a group of hang glider pilots setting up before flight. Fritz's preoccupation with the art of soaring inspired her other quilt in this chapter, *Lift-Off*.

The excitement of the early morning lift-off, the bright colors of the balloons, and the expectant faces in the crowd combine to make *Lift-Off* one of Fritz's most satisfying works.

Edward Larson, one of the pioneers who has shaped the world of contemporary pictorial quilts, has always been fascinated with the possibilities for exploring dreams and fantasies inherent in the quilt medium. Larson was so turned-on by the commission for the *Nightmare Quilt*, that he let his imagination head him into designing an enveloping stream-of-consciousness quilt.

One of the more difficult tasks confronting an artist is the necessity of integrating fantasy and reality. Lura Schwarz Smith in *Dragon Tea* has created a quilt combining the elements of fantasy with actual moments from her life. The cozy scene of a well-mannered dragon sharing a cup of tea in the artist's apartment seems absolutely believable for one split-second before reality sets in. All the quilts in this chapter are asking us to share the magic of such moments.

**LIFT-OFF**

Laura Lee Fritz (Yountville, California); 1987; 84 x 84 inches; cotton

**L***ift-Off* began with the idea to quilt a crowd scene featuring characters variously absorbed and distracted by their surroundings. I chose the balloon theme not only for my personal interest, but because it seems such a universally inspiring activity. When I attended the lift-off in Napa Valley in mid-January, I "burned" a full roll of film, shooting all stages of balloons filling and finally rising as I stood immediately below the basket of one. January didn't inspire many spectators to venture out into the frozen daybreak, so I had to wait until summer to document crowd activity. That took another roll of film. From the two rolls of photos, plus another here and there, I arranged the final composition. I even made a cameo appearance in the quilted crowd—wearing a red baseball cap.

This will be a time capsule for subsequent generations: Mom wearing a Gerry pack to carry the baby, a boy sitting on a skateboard, cowboy boots and miniskirt, shoelaces in an age of velcro kid's shoes…all signs of this time in life and probably oddities in another hundred years.

## HANG GLIDER OVER YOSEMITE

Laura Lee Fritz (Yountville, California); 1989; 71 x 76 inches; cotton

**D**riving down the coast of the Pacific Ocean over Mt. Tamalpais, I spotted three hang glider pilots setting up their kites for flight. By habit I had a camera in the car and commenced to document the process from set-up to the landings on the beach far below. When the photos returned from the shop, it was easy to select the "right" image of the glider, but the landscape wasn't as exciting in the two dimensions as it was in life. I had long desired to use Yosemite as the model for a quilt, so this was my immediate choice for the landscape, and of course, a research trip for photos.

I chose Half Dome as the focal point, viewed across the valley from the peak called Glacier Point (only after the quilt was made did I learn that Glacier Point *is* where the hang gliders launch in Yosemite Park). Keeping the mountains in perspective was a job that required a couple of weeks spent cutting shapes of color, putting them up on the felt board, deciding they didn't work and then cutting a new mountain or a new set of peaks. The sky presented another challenge: I had already quilted a plain-fabric sky in the quilt *Lift-Off*; this time I wanted an active sky. From many different blue fabrics I cut bands with hourglass curves. These bands were pieced into two large panels of many colors, then cut apart into narrow strips which were then sewed back together, first alternating the strips from panel 1 and panel 2, and then sliding the strips up and down in their places so the colors moved.

**MERRY-GO-ROUND**

Ann Johnston (Lake Oswego, Oregon); 1990; 52 x 62 inches; silk broadcloth, rhinestones, beads and fabric paint; photo by Bill Bachhuber

**M**y goal in designing this quilt was to re-create some of the splendors of the merry-go-rounds I delighted in as a small child. The magic art of the carvers combined with the glitter of lights and clamor of music made a lasting impression on me that I wanted to carry through the imagery in my quilt. In order to do this, I drew the horses from the point of view of a child looking up at them. I used a combination of carving styles and decorative harnesses for the horses, mixed in my quilt as they are mixed together in my memory. I pieced the floor in curves and used radiating lines in the ceiling to emphasize a sense of circular motion. The border quilting depicts a pipe organ accompanied by decorative elements of the era and encircled by ribbons and stars.

The quilt is made of dye painted and immersion dyed silk broadcloth. The horses are appliquéd onto the pieced and appliquéd background. It is hand and machine quilted with silk and metallic threads and embellished with rhinestones, beads and fabric paint.

The few short minutes of a merry-go-round ride provide fantasy and pleasure that lasts a long time.

**WEDDING PORTRAIT**

Margaret Cusack (Brooklyn, New York); 1983; 20 x 31 inches; satin, cotton, and fabric paint; photo by Skip Caplan

This piece was created for a friend, Tom Vacirca, as a gift for his parents on their fiftieth wedding anniversary. It was based on their wedding photograph, and although the original photo was in black and white, I chose sepia colors. I loved the strength and earnestness of the photo and enjoyed creating this fabric portrait.

The techniques include fabric collage with machine appliqué to a dyed background. Mrs. Vacirca's wedding veil was made from a transparent fabric.

**NIGHT OFFERING**

Marjorie Claybrook (Augusta, Georgia); 1991; 45 x 45 inches; cotton chintz, broadcloth, and sequins; photo by Phillip N. Jones

**W**hen I saw this fabric in a Knoxville shop, I was reminded of Gauguin's *The Offering*. In my work Polynesian women carry bowls of red stars as offerings to the night. The offering floats up to the heavens and illuminates the night sky. The blue and green sashing represents the boundaries of their island world—sky and sea. Perhaps the viewer will see the women collecting stars which fall from the night sky and think of another place and time, but in the back of his mind will be the mysteries of women, life and the universe.

*Night Offering* employs the most basic techniques of appliqué and quilting.

## SWEET SUMMER EVENING #1

Marie Combs (Kalamazoo, Michigan); 1986; 60 x 76 inches; cotton

**A** rooftop view of minarets, a summer night sky seen through the grill of a Moorish window or a mysterious doorway in old Baghdad— these and other scenes from my "Arabian Nights" quilts have been inspired by the fantasy and romance of old movies. In the 1940s and 1950s I was very interested in watching romantic movies set in the Middle East. *Kismet, The Desert Song* and *The Thief of Baghdad* were some of my favorites. The memories of those movies were what influenced my quilts. As a source for historic buildings of the Moslem world I often refer to books on Islamic Architecture. I filter and stylize images in these books through my Midwestern American vision of the Islamic world, which is based upon my childhood fantasies, remembered readings of *The Arabian Nights*, and, of course, those wonderful movies.

The lush colors I favor are balanced by subtle geometric configurations. I cut out the pieces and sew them together to achieve the nuances of color as I work and design the quilting patterns. I leave the actual quilting to a group of Amish women.

## THE NIGHTMARE QUILT

Designed by Edward Larson (Santa Fe, New Mexico) and executed by Robert and Helen Cargo, Lennie K. McCain, and Mildred Cargo
(Tuscaloosa, Alabama); 1983; 61 x 50 inches; cotton and cotton blends; courtesy of the Robert Cargo Folk Art Gallery, Tuscaloosa, Alabama

**W**hen I met Edward Larson, the well-known designer of picture quilts, some ten or twelve years ago, I commissioned him to create a quilt based on the Goya etching *The Sleep of Reason Produces Monsters*, from the *Caprichos* series. I had long been interested in the hauntingly fascinating work. Although the sleeping figure in that work is the artist, over the years he had been transformed in my mind to the scholar asleep at his work table. Larson went beyond the Spanish artist by creating a veritable hellish menagerie of horrible and threatening creatures. Serpent, cats, wolf, bat, bird, owls, a skull, a headless woman and a sinister-looking crescent-moon all swirl around a bed, appropriately covered with a crazy quilt on which writhes the sleeping person, who is obviously tortured by some terrible dream. Emerging from underneath the bed is a creature of some unearthly mixture of the plant and animal kingdoms, groping blindly towards the sleeping figure. Even the bed is not what it seems, as it appears to be metamorphosizing into a reptilian form. Up the sides of the quilt race two horses—visual puns that are labeled by the artist "Night Mare".

I particularly liked the associations Larson drew with the theme of sleep: the real quilt, the quilt depicted, the bed, the sleeping figure, the dream, the "night mares," and the pervasive nocturnal ambiance. —*Robert Cargo*

**THE FIGHT OF THE CENTURY**

Designed by Edward Larson (Santa Fe, New Mexico) and quilted by Marie Newdiger (Neosho, Missouri); 1981; 102 x 120 inches; cottons; photo by Hawthorne Studio

This is a fantasy quilt, reveling in the knockout of Muhammed Ali. At the time the quilt was started Ali was the greatest! He still is, although he's very changed from the brash poetic "spokesman" of the early years. In real life I couldn't even stand in the same gym with him, so this is a complete fantasy.

I flattened out the perspective of the image to emphasize the drama of boxing. I brought the spectators in from the border to simplify the appliquéd figures and to make the quilt direct and childlike. This is a technique I have admired in folk art; so I co-opted these concepts to achieve the desired visual.

I did work like this (drawings) before I was "educated," and it has taken me years to unlearn that education; but now I do it quite naturally—almost as if Grandma Moses was pushing my pencil. —*Edward Larson*

## ART IS SERIOUS BUSINESS

Audree L. Sells (Chaska, Minnesota); 1990; 43 x 54 inches; cotton; photo by Helen Kohler Rickman

**A**n appreciation of children's art, the Impressionists exhibit at the Minneapolis Institute of Arts and a photo by Davis Brewster were my inspirations for this quilt.

Children visiting the institute were invited to help create a mural of the Twin Cities. The event took place during the exhibit of the works of the Impressionist painters. Children, inspired by the great paintings, showed no fear as they brushed great areas of color onto the paper provided. I have always admired the spontaneous quality of children's art and their approach to it. It is with this "the child-within attitude" that I put together this piece with no fear of mistakes. It didn't have to be straight, or logical, or even explainable. As one of my second-grade students said to me when I asked him why he painted his door higher than the windows, "Because I wanted it that way."

The names and dates of Impressionist painters form the quilting design. The back is sewn with bands of primary and secondary colors. It is hand appliquéd and hand quilted.

# CHILDHOOD AND ADOLESCENCE

As a subject, the rites of childhood have interested pictorial quilters since the nineteenth century. Most early pictorials devoted to children were intended as keepsakes for close relatives and friends. Many contained blocks of patchwork interspersed with images designed to delight the nursery set. By the beginning of the twentieth century, patterns appeared in ladies' magazines and newspapers featuring appliqué designs from fairy tales, nursery rhymes, circus themes, and biblical stories. Until the advent of the art quilt in the 1970s, quilts for and about children were usually rendered in a sweet, sentimental style. The thousands of Sunbonnet Sues, Peter Pans, and Noah's Arks were conceived as utilitarian quilts for the crib or bed rather than art quilts designed for the wall. In Clovis, New Mexico, Quirl Thompson Havenhill expressed the feelings of many quilters in the early twentieth century when she reminisced about the quilts she made for her grandchildren:

> For my little girl grandbabies, I'm making quilts for their dolls and buggies. I make about six at a time with little girl things on 'em. I tell you, they're just darlin'. I do the little Sunbonnet Girl pattern a lot, and every one of them is a little different. I make some little change in the pattern. The hat or the foot turned a certain way will give each girl a personality all her own.

While many contemporary pictorial quilters are making quilts for children to enjoy, they are adding new twists. Margit Echols designed stuffed and movable parts to draw children into play activities involving her delightful *Big Apple Circus.* Other artists choose to document their children's and adolescents' lives, recreating poignant moments while commenting on milestones of social and psychological development. These quilts include "memory" quilts that pay homage to the family and treasured recollections in fabric scrapbooks such as Odette Teel's *Harry's Memory Quilt.* Many artists explore their own childhoods in their quilts, remembering the good and bad times, the games they played, and the people who shaped their lives. Whether based on reminiscence or fresh observations, children's pictorials always capture the viewer's attention with their engaging subjects and universal themes.

**CAROUSEL DREAMS**

Gloria Lynne Smith (Pleasanton, California); 1992; 64 x 94 inches; cotton

This quilt was inspired by my discovery of an exciting piece of fabric featuring carousel horses. My daughter loves horses, and when we go to Monterey, she rides the carousel all day long. She has told me about her dreams of the carousel horses. I knew she would love a quilt from this fabric for her bedroom. This is the way I see her dreaming about her carousel horses.

*Carousel Dreams* was made of machine-pieced "Attic Window" blocks. For the carousel and the little girl I used cutaway appliqué and appliqué techniques.

## GAVEN (THE GIFT)

Charlotte Warr Anderson (Salt Lake City, Utah); 1990; 24 inches in diameter; cottons, silks, 100% polyesters, sequins, and beads; photo by Borge B. Andersen & Associates, Inc.

This quilt was Grand Prize winner in the Kjeldsen's Butter Cookie Company's "Quilt a Modern Fairy Tale" contest. I made it because my in-laws are Danish and was hoping to win the trip to Denmark that was part of the Grand Prize package so that my husband could see the homeland of his parents.

The quilt shows a blue fairy hovering over a sleeping child. My daughter Aubry (whose name means "ruler of the elves") posed for the child in this quilt. The work is hand appliquéd, machine pieced and hand quilted.

## PREHISTORIC YUPPIES

Constance Scheele (Katy, Texas); 1992; 72 x 74 inches; cotton

This quilt was designed to capture the carefree freedom of youth and to relay a feeling of movement in a visual fixed form. The abstract design emphasizes this feeling of movement and requires the viewer to look for the subject matter. This is my second quilt involving this general theme. Many people responded to my first quilt, *When Twenty Seemed Old*, because they had fond memories of swinging in their childhood, as I did.

When we are children we don't realize the simple pleasures we lose as adults. This quilt is a reminder of those pleasures.

**HARRY'S MEMORY QUILT**

Odette Goodman Teel (Long Beach, California); 1990; 82 x 96 inches; cotton, cotton/poly blends, and muslin

I began this quilt as a "freedom quilt" for my son's twenty-first birthday. Harry was born in 1958, so I thought I could finish it in a year—Ha! Each block depicts something important in his life, including six immediate family portraits. Blocks feature elementary, junior high, and high school, his love of music, college degrees, favorite vacation places, and his work in the university library and in a mental health hospital.

The family portraits almost killed me—I am not a trained artist. I made the drawings from photos and anguished over them. Dad is shown in his rose garden; Mom is quilting, of course; Texas grandparents are fishing (big brother, Bruce, is telling on Harry for getting his line tangled in the tree); Bruce is also directing the orchestra; sister-in-law Nancy is wrapping a gift while her three adored cats look on; and Grandmother Nonie is treating Harry to breakfast out. Other blocks include a Corvette (the car Harry always dreamed of owning), animals that Harry loved, his very little basketball league, a motto to grow on and even the bedraggled geranium that struggled on his window shelf for years (in the quilt I made it blossom).

Harry was thirty-three when he finally received his quilt.

**HAVING FUN, WISH YOU WERE HERE**

Natasha Kempers-Cullen (Bowdoinham, Maine); 1988; 43 x 53 1/2 inches; hand painted on cotton with dyes, glass beads

This quilt is loosely based on a childhood memory of playing various board games (Checkers and Candyland) with my brother and sister while collecting postcards from interesting places my parents visited. They were both language teachers and took opportunities for educational tours in Europe and Russia. We couldn't travel with them, so the connection was only through these postcards.

### BIG APPLE CIRCUS

Margit Echols (New York, New York); 1989; 47 x 54 inches; cotton;
photo by Myron Miller

**O**f all the quilts I've made so far, *Big Apple Circus* is the one that's given me the most pleasure. I particularly enjoyed looking for books on old circus posters and then figuring out how to draw them so they'd work in patchwork and appliqué.

Even though repetition can be a restful process, making the same block over and over can be tedious. With this quilt each block was different, and I looked forward to its completion, not because it was just one more step toward the end, but because I couldn't wait to see what it would look like.

I started by making an elephant with a padded ear that moves back and forth and a banner with a hand-made tassel hat hangs loose on his side. This inspired me to design other blocks with stuffed or movable parts. Almost every one of the fifteen designs has some special feature: the seal has a padded ball; the flaps on the tent open; the aerial artist has a padded bra and hair that hangs loose; the bear's skirt is gathered and stands away from the surface of the quilt and his padded arms open out; the strong man has stuffed barbells; and the clown's jacket opens to reveal a heart.

### PRE-PUBESCENT POOL PARTY

Rebekka Seigel (Owenton, Kentucky); 1990; 110 x 88 inches; cotton and poly/cotton blends, polyester batting, cotton embroidery

**T**his quilt grew out of an experience I had as an artist-in-residence in Western Kentucky. As the school was five hours away from my home and the residency was for a month, I needed a place to stay. A friend of mine from that part of the state was gracious enough to invite me to stay in her home. I lived for that month in her ten-year-old daughter's room. On her bulletin board she had a small snapshot of her most recent birthday party which was held at the local indoor swimming pool. The guests were all lined up on the side of the pool in their bathing suits, and I was mesmerized by their budding bodies, their body language and their linear formation. I loved the photo so much that when it was time to leave, I asked the daughter if I could borrow the photo as inspiration for a quilt I would like to make. She reluctantly agreed. The young girls mostly all live around or near Paducah, Kentucky, so when the quilt was finished I sent it to the annual AQS contest and show held there each spring. It was important to me to show Danielle and her friends what I had done with their images. The quilt won second prize in the professional appliqué category. The techniques involved are appliqué for the figures and machine piecing for most of the rest of the quilt. It is all hand quilted.

## MOUNTAIN DOLLMAKER

Rebekka Seigel (Owenton, Kentucky); 1989; 39 x 34 inches; cotton fabrics (many from the 1930s and 1940s given to me by a student); photo by Jay Bachemin

**T**his quilt is the third in a series of pieces I made for a show in the mountains of eastern Kentucky. I wanted to do some portraits of mountain people against quilt patterns that are indigenous to the region. While working in eastern Kentucky as an artist-in-residence, I was struck by the strong role that quiltmaking still plays in the lives of the people there. The children all told me that they had quilts at home that were made for them by their "mammaws." When the children and I invited the parents and grandparents to visit the school for a show-and-tell day, there wasn't an empty seat in the room and the pride that each of the quiltmakers exhibited was very touching.

The woman featured on this quilt is taken from a Doris Ulmann photograph made in the late 1920s or early 1930s as she traveled through the Appalachian mountains with her camera. The woman's name is Mrs. Green Williams and she is simply described as a doll-maker. I do not know where she was from. This quilt is my favorite one of the series.

**PUZZLED BEAZ**

Kathy Jevne Clark (Euless, Texas); 1991; 36 1/2 x 33 1/2 inches; cotton and beads; photo by David Larsen

**P**uzzled Beaz is one of my favorite quilts. Each of the goldfish seem to have personalities all their own. One goldfish seems snobbish, another looks intelligent, while my favorite appears ready to be friends with anyone who walks by the fish bowl.

An old torn-up puzzle box designed by Joan Luby provided the inspiration for Puzzled Beaz. We named the quilt after a goldfish given to us by a friend, which received its name from the Mrs. Beasley of the Reggie and Jughead comic strip. Because the idea came from a puzzle box and the goldfish was called Beaz for short, the quilt became Puzzled Beaz.

Since each piece in the quilt is a different size and shape, there was no fast way of piecing it. I used my version of freezer paper piecing, making this quilt one of my biggest challenges to date. It is not only non-typical of the way I usually construct pieces but is also very different in style from my other work. To finish the quilt I added beads in three sizes to give the appearance of bubbles floating to the top of the bowl.

# A NIMALS

The legacy of animals in pictorial quilts celebrates creatures of the wild and their domestic counterparts. Quilt artists of the eighteenth and nineteenth centuries, surrounded by animals in rural settings, sewed their observations into quilts that featured primitive, folky animals drawn from daily life. In the larger towns more formal renditions of animals were favored in the stylized Broderie Perse counterpanes and Baltimore Album quilts. Quilters who very likely had never traveled more than thirty miles from home pored over books and magazines, dreaming of exotic animals in faraway places. They often relied on engravings to help them depict animals they had never actually seen.

Today quilt artists living in a world of television and fax machines are more concerned about communicating their personal visions through their art than they are in depicting animals for the edification of their audience. They are likely to be interested in portraying animals as part of a divine plan, or defining animals in terms of the human condition, or simply expressing their love for a favorite pet or a particular species.

The variety of today's pictorial animal quilts manifests an impressive energy. Artists such as Montana's Nancy Erickson explore animals' psyches as well as their physical attributes. Often an animal will appear in many guises in various pieces before Erickson has worked it out of her system. Whether she chooses to portray rabbits, lions, ravens, or rodents, she acknowledges her subjects as powerful elements in life, believing they "act as familiars, or spiritual guides, in the lives of humans." Noting that lions in the wild pay no attention to the human condition, as they are too busy being involved in their own time-honored activities; Erickson quotes from a poem, "Boats in a Fog," by Robinson Jeffers to communicate what she feels about animals and her art:

> ...all the arts lose virtue
> Against the essential reality
> Of creatures going about their business among the equally
> Earnest elements of nature.

A number of artists specializing in animal quilts are fascinated with the animals depicted in the cave art of ancient times. The art of Native Americans and Africans, replete with animal images, are incorporated into quilts of stunning intensity. Barbara Moore, a Vermont artist, speaks for many quilts artists when she says she "feels fortunate in being able to integrate my love and knowledge of wild mammals into most areas of my professional life." Quilt artist, Iris Gowan acknowledges the debt her quilts owe to her upbringing in Africa, where she observed firsthand the many species of animal life.

Perhaps the preoccupation with animals by many of America's most noted quilt artists can best be explained with a quote by an Indian Chief: "What good is man without beasts?...If all the beasts were gone, man would die from a great loneliness of spirit." I think all the artists in this chapter would certainly agree with him.

**SMILES**

Marjorie Claybrook (Augusta, Georgia); 1986; 45 x 40 inches; cotton chintz, sateen, broadcloth, batik, sequins, and Ultrasuede; photo by Phillip N. Jones

I am a fan of pop culture, especially music videos. *Miami Vice* was the first television show (since Ernie Kovacs) to employ music with images as an integral part of the production. The flamingos rushing across the screen during the titles was the inspiration for this work. *The Flamingo's Smile* by Stephen Gould, which was published during this period, deals with animal adaptation—the beak takes its unique shape and perennial smile from the mode of feeding upside down.

*Smiles* also represents a transition from works more formally organized to free-form appliqué and reverse appliqué with generous use of embroidery and sequins. Fabric for this quilt was purchased by my husband in Washington, D.C. He always takes time on business trips to prospect for unusual fabrics for my work.

**THE WRESTLERS**

Nancy Erickson (Missoula, Montana); 1989; 63 x 45 inches; cotton, velvet, and satin; photo by Nancy Erickson

In Kafka's diaries, somewhere, is a tale of a lone man in a room who hears a tap at the door. He answers the door, gestures for the caller, another man, to come in, and they wrestle silently, vigorously, for an hour. At the end of that period, exactly, the visitor leaves, as silently as he came. For some odd reason this odd tale worked its way into this piece. Cats do wrestle endlessly, especially those who are good friends.

Technically, I wanted to use this jolting orange velvet, with red paint, and to make the piece free-form, free of Renaissance space indications. The eyes gazing outward with the lavender stain were the surprise—they stay with me now, four years later, although the piece resides with someone else. Subsequently, I did three more lion-wrestling works, introducing space and the figure again, but this was the only one with the unusual all-seeing eyes.

**ALPHA-BESTIARY**

Jo Diggs (Portland, Maine); 1991; 120 x 96 inches; cottons, cotton blends, and synthetic fabrics; photo by Jay York

In a competition of the "Percent for Arts Project" for the Prides Corner School in Westbrook, Maine, I was chosen to create the *Alpha-Bestiary* quilt to decorate a new addition to the building. The quilt shows a deep, dark forest opening out to great, light vistas, suggesting expanding horizons through learning. In the forest are all the letters of the alphabet with animals whose names start with matching letters. Some of these animals and letters are fairly hard to find, presenting a challenge for the children. In designing the quilt I remembered how much fun I had as a child trying to find the hidden animals or objects in the puzzles in various children's magazines.

*Alpha-Bestiary* represented a big sale, an excuse to buy new fabrics (and to use up some old ones), the joy of meeting the staff and children of a really special school, the hard but enjoyable labor of stitching for two months, and the final pleasure of the presentation day. The quilt became part of the educational process of the school. A video showing me working on the quilt helped the children learn about quilts and quilting. I visited the school and talked to all the classes about the history of quilts and their care. *Alpha-Bestiary* hangs open to all (no glass) in the main entry hall.

The quilt was appliquéd by hand with minimal hand quilting composed of long diagonal lines. It was designed on a wall but stitched on a table after I finished the layout. It is worked from center out in all directions, one layer at a time. When the top layer was finished, I cut away underlapped areas to prevent the quilt from becoming too bulky or heavy.

**BRIGHT VISIONS**

Barbara Pettings Moore (Shelburne, Vermont); 1987; 89 x 89 inches; Ultrasuede facile, and broadcloth; collection of Mrs. Kendall Mix

**O**ld-world prehistoric cave and rock art, the theme of this quilt, was suggested by the owner who commissioned it. Her preference was a delightful one for the artist who has a great affection for mammals. The research-directed following months were so educationally rich that designing the quilt became "an independent study of Paleolithic art history." The title, *Bright Visions*, came about in an almost prophetic way. As the quilt, still nameless, neared completion, an exhibit entitled "Dark Caves: Bright Visions" opened at the Museum of Natural History in New York City. Visitors entered this collection of prehistoric art and artifacts from Western Europe by walking through a darkened hallway lined with photographs and enormous serigraphs (hand-screened prints) of cave art. At first *Bright Visions* was one of several title options: over time it seemed the only appropriate choice.

The quilt's large central panel is an appliquéd reproduction of the Hall of Bulls in Lascaux Cave, Dordogne, France. Half the animal figures in the squares surrounding it are adapted from paintings and engravings in French and Spanish caves. The hand-sewn Ultrasuede animals in the remaining eight squares are copies of prehistoric North African art, found on the undersides of rock shelters nestled into an arid and hard-to-reach plateau in the Atlas Mountains. These are among the oldest surviving examples of rock art in Africa. The animal-cracker-like border figures are a mixture of African and European motifs. Some are shown upside-down in a manner used to depict death by primitive artists throughout much of the world.

**LIFE IN THE JUNGLE**

Iris Marie Gowen (Astoria, New York); 1991; 36 x 63 inches; cotton; photo by Myron Miller

I spent most of my childhood and a significant portion of my adult life living in Africa. This quilt serves both as an expression of some memories of that early time, and as a warning of the threat posed by man to life in the jungle.

The quilt offers a view of various aspects of jungle life—abundant birds, animals, and plants. The formalized structure of the block design (a version of the classic "Attic Windows" pattern) focuses the eye on the animals within the centered squares. Most of the wildlife prints are of African origin; their vitality and color contrast with the more formal geometric designs on the "windows" in which they are contained.

I chose to use all patterned prints in this quilt. As in the rainforest itself, the observer's eye has no solid blocks of color on which to rest, but must move constantly, from one pattern to another, trying to make sense of everything at once. The colors are all of a similar tone, with occasional lighter shades to echo the shafts of blazing sun which burst into the dark underbrush. The border and sashing fabric frames the blocks with foliage, increasing in density as it moves away from the center to the shadows at the edge of the forest canopy.

The central squares of the quilt suggests the future of most jungle life. The cooking pots are not only ominous in themselves, but they are surrounded by rows of eggs and peanuts, foreshadowing the cultivation which follows when man has displaced or consumed the wild animals.

**COURAGE**

Therese May (San Jose, California); 1990; 29 x 34 inches; mixed fabrics, acrylic paint

Often when I am working, my supposed goal is really someone else's idea. When I started this piece, it was for a show with chairs as a theme. Of course chairs were the furthest thing from my mind, but I made a little image of a chair, anyway. Then I built out from there using imagery that was closer to the way I really felt (little smiling dogs with teeth), and later the all-knowing cat was added with paint. Then, I wrote the word "COURAGE" across the top—an affirmation of encouragement to all people—a way of saying, "Lets go for it!" It is a reminder to stay centered and positive.

**OH, THE COW'S OUT AGAIN!**

Sue Holdaway-Heys (Ann Arbor, Michigan); 1989; 56 x 56 inches; cottons, cotton blends, acrylic paints, embroidery and markers; photo by Bernie O'Brien

This quilt was inspired by my love of barns. I had painted barns in watercolor for years and constantly took photos of interesting barns throughout the Midwest. The barn represents to me an American institution which seems more and more distant to the lifestyle of the majority of Americans. I am fascinated with the idea of acres of land around me, animals, crops, and big machinery. I am a "city girl" and probably always will be—but something draws me to the barn structure.

Using acrylics I painted the large scene of the barn, cut it up, and rearranged the pieces, placing the painted fabric in areas throughout the quilt. The field is embellished with stitched wheat and grasses. The cow has been given more detail with permanent marker. I wanted to draw the viewer into the scene and decided to have the cow wander off outside the grazing field.

# RURAL SCENES

Rural scenes, a favorite subject of pictorial quilters, have always delighted the public. As American as apple pie, these quilts call up feelings of nostalgia for the idylls of rural life. In this chapter some of the most evocative quilts were made by artists living in big cities, yearning for a simpler time and place. As Sally Sellers notes, many of us idealize the concept of "a home with a picket fence and rose garden," although "few of us actually live in houses like this…yet this is how we represent our concept of home." Although Wendy Huhn admits a part of her "longs for the big city and bright lights," she celebrates the joys of the country in a series of bucolic quilts starring a group of winsome cows. Sue Holdaway-Heys in *Oh, the Cow's Out Again* highlights another rural American institution, the barn. Calling herself a "city girl," she notes her fascination with barns, having spent years photographing and painting them before attempting to capture their essence in a pictorial quilt.

Quilts focusing on rural themes are frequently memory quilts, depicting scenes recalled from childhood or based on faded, family photographs of homesteads, town landmarks, and scenic views. Rosie Morgan and Robert Cargo chose to document the small town America of the nineteenth and early twentieth centuries, providing "an intimate glimpse into the life of pioneer families." Nora Ezell's *Jones Valley Quilt* memorializes her childhood days in rural Alabama, combining handed-down quilting patterns with images of home, church and school. Ezell taught herself to quilt more than forty years ago by watching her mother and aunt work on their scrap quilts. Dottie Moore, maker of *Appalachian Afternoon,* wishes to re-create memories of sites along the Appalachian Trail. To achieve "the essence of a memory" she relies on her intuition to forge a bond between the emerging quilt and a remembered image.

Although the subject matter of rural scenes is traditional, the techniques employed by today's artists reflect contemporary aesthetics. A sophisticated approach utilizing the principles of abstraction and the juxtaposition of diverse elements within a cohesive framework mark the best of these works. Artists in this chapter consider themselves colorists, using freely the myriad hues of the vegetative countryside. At the heart of this chapter are seasonal images, suggesting an underlying preoccupation with life cycles of birth and renewal.

**JONES VALLEY QUILT**

Nora Ezell (Greene County, Alabama); 1987; 94 x 71 inches; cotton and cotton blends; courtesy of the Robert Cargo Folk Art Gallery, Tuscaloosa, Alabama

**S**eventy-four-year-old Nora Ezell was born and grew up in Birmingham, Alabama, known in the early days as Jones Valley. This quilt is a memory piece that preserves Ezell's recollections of her early years there. In an exhibition at the Birmingham Public Library in 1990 the quilt was reviewed by art critic, James Nelson who wrote in the *Birmingham News*: "In the *Jones Valley Quilt* Ms. Ezell recalls her Fairfield [a Birmingham suburb] past with home, church, school and mill nestled in a picture-pretty site framed by various abstract designs." In the same review Ezell is quoted as follows concerning her work: "I like my ideas. I do whatever comes from the top of my head. Crazy or creative—you be the judge."

In 1989 two quilts made by Nora Ezell were included in the exhibition "Stitching Memories: African-American Story Quilts," Williams College, Williamstown, Massachusetts. In 1990 as the recipient of the Alabama Folk Heritage Award, she was described as "a quiltmaker of extraordinary talent and commitment as well as an articulate spokeswoman for an art form that is deeply rooted in Alabama culture.

---

**THE THOMAS FAMILY QUILT**

Top made by Rosie Morgan (Cullman, Alabama), quilted by Robert Cargo (Tuscaloosa, Alabama); 1982 (quilted 1991); 63 x 67 inches; cotton, cotton blends and lace; courtesy of the Robert Cargo Folk Art Gallery, Tuscaloosa, Alabama

In 1982 in a fabric store in Cullman, Alabama, I saw on display a quilt that had been made by Rosie Morgan, a clerk in the shop. It depicted a church in the Cullman area, and at once I thought of the possibility of having the maker do a quilt based on the Thomas family

photograph showing my great-grandmother, my grandparents, and other relatives standing in front of their quilt-draped porch in 1899. (The photograph offers an intimate glimpse into the unadorned and simple life of a pioneer family in remote Alabama at the very end of the nineteenth century, as well as being a remarkable, if not unique, piece of documentation of nineteenth-century quilts and persons.) [1]

Mrs. Morgan agreed to make the top; my mother, Mildred Thomas Cargo, embroidered the faces on the various figures. The top remained unquilted until 1991 when I quilted it. Except for a few church pieces, it is the only picture quilt Rosie Morgan, an accomplished quiltmaker, has made.—*Robert Cargo*

1. Quoted in *The Quilt Digest*, no. 3, San Francisco: The Quilt Digest Press, 1985, p. 63.

**BREATH OF EUGENE**

Midge Hoffman (Eugene, Oregon); 1991; 80 x 120 inches; linen, chintz, and cotton canvas; collection of the Allergy and Asthma Associates, P.C., Eugene, Oregon; photo by Paul Neevel

**B**reath of Eugene was commissioned for the two-story lobby wall of an allergy and asthma clinic and represents a collaborative effort by the artist, the doctors, and the interior designer.

The doctors are avid runners and wanted to portray this interest. I felt that office visitors could benefit from reflecting on the positive attributes of our community and the effort involved in staying healthy—in spite of some of the local environmental hazards that may have contributed to the need of an office visit.

Runners can be seen in all weather conditions, on the streets and on the many trails throughout Eugene, as well as on rural country roads surrounding the city. This piece depicts the familiar sites seen "on the run": the rhododendrons and forests of fir trees, the McKenzie and Willamette rivers, the Cascade Mountains in the distance, the diverse blend of architecture and culture represented by two familiar structures. The cool colors, blues and greens, are my "Northwest colors."

## HOMEBODY

Sally A. Sellers (Vancouver, Washington); 1992; 59 x 56 inches; cottons, synthetics, lurex, lamé, velvet, metallics, and canvas

**H**omebody emerged from my continuing fascination with windows, houses, and the concept of home. One of the first representational icons that children draw is the standard house-with-door-and-chimney. It is an instantly recognizable image in several cultures. It is also an immensely appealing image, especially combined with a picket fence (which is itself an echo of the house shape). Few of us actually live in houses like this in idyllic rural settings, yet this is how we represent our concept of home.

Very similar to the simplified house symbol is the representation of a woman as a triangle with a circle above and two vertical rectangles below. This is surely more than a coincidence. This similarity, along with her idea that our homes are, in reality, extensions of ourselves, generated the *Homebody* title and the dual image.

To portray this dwelling with square corners and correct alignment would be to rob it of its humanity. I wanted to portray it as my daughter would draw it—full of emotion and vitality, wonderfully askew—as is our own home.

## BESSY, BOSSY, FLO AND A FRIEND VISIT THE FARM

Wendy C. Huhn (Dexter, Oregon); 1988; 30 x 46 inches; cottons and color transfers; collection of the Eugene Water & Electric Board, Eugene, Oregon

**T**his is the second quilt that I made for my "Traveling Cow" series. "The girls" have since traveled the world. They are my alter egos. For them it was a return to their birthplace. A part of me adores the rural life—which I live now—and the other part longs for the big city and bright lights.

The work was hand quilted, machine pieced, and employed color transfers.

**APPALACHIAN AFTERNOON**

Dottie Moore (Rock Hill, South Carolina); 1991; 62 x 70 inches; cotton and cotton blends; photo by Mike Harrison

**A**ppalachian Afternoon is my way of bringing the mystery and secrets of the mountains and trees into a visual form. The Appalachian Trail crosses a peak in North Carolina called Max Patch, a place I have visited many times. Alone at Match Patch the world opens, and the mountains speak. I like the way the Appalachian Trail flows across the top of Max Patch. I wonder about the people who have walked the trail, about their hopes and dreams. This art quilt was conceived from the feelings and memories of this special place.

Appalachian Afternoon was created without a sketch. I began by simply moving fabric around until the piece started to take form. I cut the shapes from cloth without the use of patterns. The tree emerged from some chalk lines drawn directly onto the fabric. My best pieces flow from a place without words. The hardest part is trusting my intuition, focusing on my feelings while trying to remove the obstacles that obstruct the essence of a memory. It's difficult to move beyond doubts because the ego wants to control. I can't think of a piece that hasn't created fears of failure, but the many hours invested in each one help me to move beyond these fears to the complete art quilt. The hand embroidery is the final step and the most important. It is when I add embroidery detail that the piece comes alive.

## BEGINNINGS I AND II (DIPTYCH)

Erika Carter (Bellevue, Washington); 1991; each 54 1/2 x 65 inches; cotton fabric, cotton classic batting

**B**eginnings I and II was commissioned by Swedish Hospital, Seattle, for their maternity ward. I chose to design a diptych of a typical Pacific Northwest spring in natural colors. Spring imagery seemed appropriate for the maternity floor, symbolizing the season of rebirth. However, two other reasons also played a part. Initially I thought a quilt in two parts could solve the physical problems of a piece long enough for the space, but I also decided to subtly suggest a male and female side, the male on the left with its strong vertical lines of the pine tree trunks and the female on the right with the soft curving lines of a flowering tree. To tie the two together, rhododendrons, ferns, and rocks appear on both pieces. Another, more private, reason I felt motivated to design a diptych was because my two children, a son and a daughter, were both born in the spring at Swedish Hospital.

The quilt is hand appliquéd and hand quilted. I first designed the background of strips on a wall. After the background was sewn together by machine, the foreground was composed and hand appliquéd in place. I chose to hand quilt this piece because I felt the broken line of hand stitching was a better aesthetic choice than the hard edge machine quilting produces.

**OLE MAN CHRISTMAS**

Kathy Jevne Clark (Euless, Texas); 1991; 47 3/4 x 64 inches; cottons, lamé, fringe, holly leaves and stuffed berries; photo by Davis Larsen

**C**hristmas has always been a special time for me. When I saw a tin with this design by Mary Engelbreit, I knew it would be my next project as I always wanted to make a Christmas quilt and Mary Engelbreit is one of my favorite artists.

The quilt was constructed using freezer paper as a template. The fabric selection came fairly easily though I did not choose traditional Christmas colors. There is very little red in the quilt—orange is used as the primary color with only a touch of green as an accent. The pants are made of red lamé with a 100% cotton cross-weave in black, and the hat is the same fabric but in gold. The sky fabric was found long before this project was started—it was a Laura Ashley fabric that I could not resist. It was cut (I should say chopped) with a child's paper scissors. The saleslady was mad when I asked her to cut the fabric instead of tearing it. To the sack fabric I added holly leaves and stuffed berries to give a three dimensional effect. Fringe that hangs freely to provide an illusion of motion completes the scarf.

The quilt turned out to be a contemporary rendition of Santa Claus, but it still is able to tug at the memories of long ago. Hopefully, it will become a part of our family's Christmas traditions.

# **H** OLIDAYS

Joyous holiday pictorials document special times. Many holiday quilts are Christmas quilts incorporating traditional symbols such as holly and candles. Childhood visions of Christmas—including Santa Claus, candy canes, gingerbread men, stockings, and reindeer—are just a few of the many popular motifs appearing in these quilts.

In 1989, the House of Fabrics inaugurated an annual contest, "Season's Greetings," which in 1991 had 250 entries. In other holiday quilts artists re-create scenes of small-town America from parades celebrating the Fourth of July to children trick-or-treating on Halloween. In a different vein there are contemporary artists poking gentle fun at time-honored traditions in unorthodox quilts. Wendy Huhn in *And the Skulls Were There That Grinned at Me* plays upon the macabre aspects of Halloween. Her quilt becomes a medium through which she attempts to deal with intimations of mortality while she is playing with traditional images of the holiday. Whether tongue-in-cheek or straightforward the quilts of this section truly commemorate the holidays and moments that enrich our lives in styles replete with symbolism both seen and suggested.

### TRICK OR TREAT

Linda Denner (Garden City, New York); 1990; 40 1/2 x 41 inches; cotton

**T***rick or Treat* attempts to capture the spirit of Halloween, one of America's favorite holidays. The sky is executed in a kaleidoscope pattern while the figures and scenery are hand pieced and/or hand appliquéd. To add to the liveliness of the piece I have embellished the image with miniatures, toys, buttons, and embroidery. Laser-cut spiderwebs are sewn to the surface to accent the house, and the tombstones are embroidered with the date and initials of the quilt-maker. *Trick or Treat* is machine quilted.

### FOURTH OF JULY

Linda Denner (Garden City, New York); 1991; 39 x 42 inches; cotton and lamé

**T**aken from a photo of a hometown street, this scene celebrates the grassroots pride and nationalism that is at the root of every American town. The sky is a pieced unit of the traditional "Storms-At-Sea" quilt pattern. The houses and/or storefronts are entirely pieced; the figures are hand embroidered with inked features; and the band carries sewn-down miniature instruments.

The border is composed of a crazy-patch motif—made of red, white, and blue fabrics assembled in a random composition. The construction is representative of the American character—random, arbitrary at times but uniquely American. The border is embellished with political campaign buttons.

The backing of *Fourth of July* is a pieced American flag. To maintain the integrity of the front and back design elements the quilt is quilted with clear nylon thread (both top and bobbin threads).

## AND THE SKULLS WERE THERE THAT GRINNED AT ME

Wendy C. Huhn (Dexter, Oregon); 1991; 33 x 35 inches; cotton, cotton blends, beads, and fabric paint

This work is one in a series of quilts that celebrate Halloween, my favorite holiday. Skulls are a recurring image in my work, representing both life and death. Perhaps this is my way of dealing with my own mortality—with a twist of humor.

As I worked on this quilt I thought about a favorite poem of mine, "A Dance with Death" by Luisa Re Mondini and the title of the quilt comes from a line in the poem.

> I danced a dance with Death last night—
> We did the swiftest glide.
> I started with my partner, Death,
> Upon a mountain side.
> We danced and danced together,
> Until the first dawn showed.
> We danced the dance, Endurance,
> Until the world awoke.
> Then, looking down the mountain side,
> I lost my step!
> My partner, Death, was guiding me
> Down to a blackened pit—
> A horrible deep pit!
> And the skulls were there that grinned at me,
> And finger bones that beckoned me to come.

The techniques used in making this quilt include machine piecing, hand and machine quilting, and polymer transfers.

## WE GIVE THANKS

Charlotte Warr Anderson (Salt Lake City, Utah); 1986; 26 x 26 inches; cottons; courtesy of the LDS Museum of Church History and Art, Salt Lake City, Utah; photo by Ronald Read

The center block of this quilt was originally meant to be part of my Statue of Liberty Centennial quilt. The idea I was working on was not turning out, so I put this block, along with the others I had made, aside and started something else. Later, the director of the LDS Hospital Quilt Auction asked me to make a quilt for their annual event. I went back to this block, surrounded it with cornucopias, sheaves of wheat and a placard, and donated it to the auction.

**TWELFTH NIGHT TALLY**

Jodi G. Warner (South Jordan, Utah); 1992; 65 x 94 inches; cotton; photo by Borge B. Andersen & Associates, Inc.

**C**hristmas, as an artist's inspiration, may be unsurpassed. It has the enchanting quality of seeming to be a once-in-a-lifetime event which happily is repeated on a yearly basis. An all-out expenditure of time and effort is justified since special creations can be enjoyed again and again.

From seeds undoubtedly sowed in my childhood fondness for the magic and music of Christmas, "The Twelve Days of Christmas" theme grew into a personal challenge to design a quilt with *every one* of the figures mentioned in the lyrics. What evolved was the pyramid shape of a Christmas tree, the inevitable result of the increase of figures from one to twelve. As the outline developed, some totally enjoyable research was necessary to compare interpretations of the Twelve Days figures and activities. These findings, plus a personal relish for European folk traditions, led to depicting some of the days in nontraditional ways. There is a Partridge in a potted topiary pear tree, Lords-a-Leaping on horseback during a fox hunt, Ladies Dancing in traditional Swedish celebration of St. Lucia Day, and Pipers Piping fanfare horns and pipe organs. Tallied, the fifty people and thirty-nine animals in the central panel create enough visual noise to delight any child of Christmas. But there remains at least one more discovery to be made: an extra, hidden figure not mentioned in the carol. In the spirit of *Where's Waldo?* look closely to find that the interloper is the red fox pursued by the hunters in the bottom row. So casual is the chase that he is at leisure to cast a rather greedy eye on the many fowl around him.

**CALICO CHRISTMAS**

Margaret Cusack (Brooklyn, New York); 1987; 12 x 15 inches; cottons and trimmings; photo by Skip Caplan

Calico Christmas was created as an illustration for *Parents* magazine. The article was about a family who enjoyed Christmas *so* much that they didn't mind the commercialization of the holiday season, with Christmas hoopla appearing earlier each year. I guess, I am also a Christmas aficionado and am willing to sing carols in July at the drop of a hat! I liked the folk-art quality in this piece and the pattern-on-pattern repeat.

Techniques include fabric collage with machine quilting. The clouds are dyed, and the border is woven rick-rack that I'd bought years ago because I thought it was charming.

**CALENDAR QUILT**

Jennie Chestnut (Louisville, Kentucky); cotton; courtesy of Laura Fisher Antiques, New York, New York

**P**robably designed for a child's bedroom, this quilt features the holiday of the month set in traditional blocks. For months lacking major holidays the quilter depicted a characteristic of the month such as April showers.

**SKYLINE PIGEON**

Karen Felicity Berkenfeld (New York, New York); 1991; 50 x 54 inches; cotton; courtesy of Barbara Ranta; photo by Karen Bell

**S**kyline Pigeon celebrates New York and her people through bright, free-form pigeons soaring over an immovable skyline, shown in subdued blues and grays. The title is from a song by Elton John that was closely associated with Ryan White, the young boy who died of AIDS.

The quilt is composed of approximately ninety percent hand-printed fabrics. The images and patterns are printed with carved linoleum blocks and textile paints on white cotton. Some of the background areas are stenciled and sponge painted. Skyline Pigeons was exhibited in the "Citiquilts" show at the Great American Quilt Festival.

# URBAN ENVIRONMENTS

It is not so long ago that the concept of an "urban" quilt would have raised a few eyebrows. Quilting was thought of as a rural calling that depended on idyllic pastoral scenes for inspiration. Today some of the most active quilting networks, including the prestigious Manhattan Quilters Guild, are in metropolitan centers. Their members win increasing numbers of awards in national contests and are represented in many quilters' magazines and books. Since the resurgence of quilting in the 1970s, urban quilters have chosen to celebrate the joys of living in the fast lane as well as record the frazzled nerves and horrors of city life.

Citiscapes have added a new dimension to pictorial quilting, focusing on subjects seldom seen until recently. Artists such as Dee Danley-Brown capture the topography of the city, re-creating sensuous urban scenes of picture-postcard beauty. Her work examines the way we view buildings: from a distance, from the street, from the windows of other buildings. "The city becomes quilt-like in terms of repeated geometric forms. Since I moved to New York, I'd been collecting black-and-white fabrics, and I finally realized why I was doing it." Danley-Brown, Marie Wilson, Yvonne Foreman, and Marguerite Malwitz, like many urban quilters, are fascinated with small architectural details of buildings as well as panoramic vistas. They zero in on these decorative ele-

ments as integral parts of their work. Whether it is a pediment of a nineteenth-century building, a sculpture adorning a skyscraper, a mosaic tile from a subway station, or a Santa Fe window sill—each forms part of the urban tapestry.

Urban quilts reflect the *Yin* and the *Yang* of the city. By defining the chaos and order of city life, artists can achieve a sense of control over the unpredictable. Deborah Anderson focuses on a demolition site in Columbus, Ohio, while Barbara Watler confronts urban crime; both artists are dealing with painful subjects more common on the pages of a newspaper than in the stitches of a quilt.

Some artists celebrate the unique "happenings" of the quintessential urban center, New York City, by illustrating its popular folklore and spectacular views. Marie Wilson's and Vikki Chenette's vignettes of the city reveal a love affair with American world capital. Even the ubiquitous bird in Karen Berkenfeld's *Skyline Pigeons* metamorphoses into a soaring paean to Manhattan.

Many viewers consider urban quilts among the most exciting interpretations of the contemporary scene. Artists are inventing a new vocabulary within the medium, adding the rich imagery of the urban landscape to an established American heritage of scenic quilts.

**CANAL STREET**

Yvonne Forman (New York, New York); 1989; hand quilted by Grace Miller; 73 x 88 inches; cotton

In 1904 August Belmont, financier of New York City's first subway line, conceived of and funded the beautiful terra-cotta mosaic tiles and bas reliefs that are mounted on the walls of many of the system's subway stations. His intention was that these decorative motifs serve both to beautify the subterranean environment as well as to help orient the many illiterate immigrants as to their whereabouts. Eight decades later these many hued, hand-cut ceramics, jeopardized by dirt, disrepair and the harsh environment of an overstressed system, have become the inspiration for a series I have entitled "Quilts from the NY Subways." These quilts satisfy my desire not only to testify to the beauty of these tiny endangered voices, but to preserve this beauty for a wider public.

Guided by my Mennonite upbringing, the translation of these designs into traditional quilting materials and techniques was a natural one for me. The techniques used in the ties moved easily from hard to soft: the geometric mosaic designs to patchwork, the hand-cut pictures mosaics to appliqué, and the bas relief to trapunto. The challenge has been to convert these beloved landmarks from ceramic to fiber without compromising the integrity of either the mosaics or the traditional quilt.

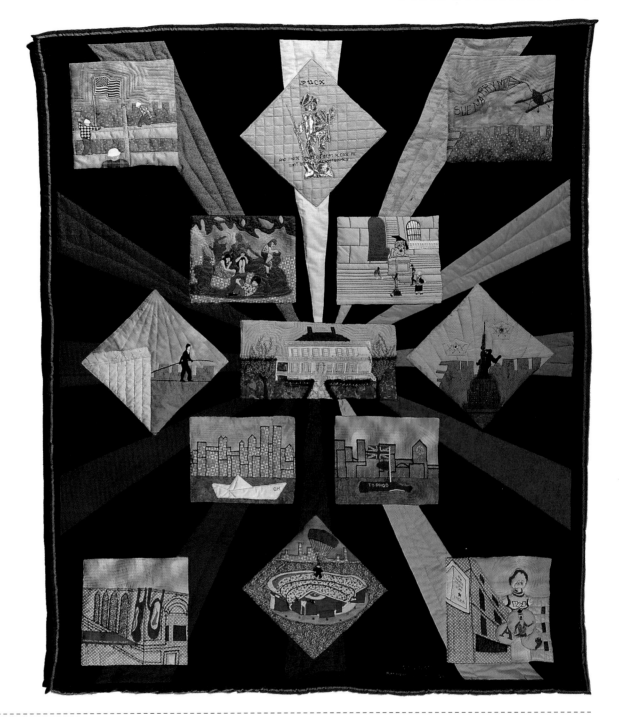

**HIGH JINKS**

Marie Wilson (New York, New York); 1991; 60 x 74 inches; cotton and cotton blends

**N**ew York City is much more than a geographical location. It is a state of mind and a "happening." Nothing seems too strange to happen here. I love it! *High Jinks* is a fond memoir of pranks and events that have been recorded here in our recent history.

The waters around New York actually hosted a "paper" folded boat and a boat shaped like a bottle. Someone did walk a tightrope between the towers of the World Trade Center. An inflated, plastic King Kong was hoisted to the top of the Empire State Building to mark the 50th anniversary of the movie *King Kong*. During the 1986 World Series, a fan parachuted into Shea Stadium waving a banner saying "Lets Go Mets." The color wheel radiating from the center symbolizes my feeling that the city is for everyone. Gracie Mansion is where mayors of New York City live. Another block, "Topping Out," depicts the ceremony that marks the installation of the highest beam in a skyscraper's framework—ironworkers place an American flag and an evergreen tree on the beam, thereby bringing new life into the building. Other blocks include a portrait of the Puck Building at 295 Lafayette Street, a famous statue of Alice In Wonderland located in Central Park, a thirty-foot inflatable sculpture of The Red Shoes that in 1986 hung from the roof of the Brooklyn Academy of Music, and a scene from the Thanksgivingday Parade.

To make this quilt I have employed appliqué embellished with embroidery and quilting.

## SANTA FE WINDOWS

Marguerite Malwitz (Brookfield, Connecticut); 1992; 55 x 62 1/2 inches; cotton, silk, linen, buttons, and beads; photo by Brad Stanton

**S**anta Fe Windows was inspired by a trip to Santa Fe where I was truly challenged as a fiber artist to be more aggressive in my approach to color. Although the landscape and architecture of the area were *so* brown, the streets and galleries were alive with color! I was particularly taken with the glorious use of rich sky blue and turquoise paint on the ornately carved window trim and doors against the adobe backdrop.

Inspired by what I saw in Santa Fe, I chose to explore the window theme and continue my design interest in the cactus motif. The pictorial quilt I created is a three-layer, dimensionally visual landscape: first, the large ornately trimmed Santa Fe Window superimposed over the total quilt image; second, the Saguaro cactus appears beyond the window; and third, a Santa Fe-style street scene appears through the window. To the left and right of the street scene and beyond the window frame are images of the outskirts of town—a tree beyond a wall and pinion covered hills.

*Santa Fe Windows* incorporated the hardest design to translate into fabric and represented a lesson in problem solving involving a number of techniques including machine and hand piecing, hand and machine appliqué, hand and machine quilting, strip piecing (the cactus) and fabric-covered cording (the running lengths of the window frame).

**PEELING THE BIG APPLE: THE VIEW FROM JERSEY CITY**

Vikki Berman Chenette (Jersey City, New Jersey); 1989; 40 x 45 inches; cotton with acrylic paint

I made this quilt in 1989 for the "Quilts for an Urban Landscape" exhibit at the New York City Department of Parks and Recreation's Arsenal Gallery. I wanted to make an album-type of appliqué quilt with city scenes.

Although my home is very close to Manhattan with scenic views of the skyline and its landmark buildings, I have to cross the Hudson River by train, tunnel, or ferry to get there. Some images had become so familiar that they worked themselves into the quilt. The scenes portray the skyline as seen from Jersey City, an approach to the Holland tunnel, a Path subway train station, and the ever-present homeless people. It was difficult to determine how to present these images until I had the idea of the cross-section of the "Big Apple" and its undulating peel.

This quilt gave me the opportunity to combine some very unusual fabrics collected over the years with several techniques: appliqué, piecing, curved seam piecing by hand and machine, and painting. It also afforded me the vehicle to come to terms with moving back to my home-town area after a decade spent in New England.

**GRID LIGHT**

Dee Danley-Brown (Westbrook, Connecticut); 1990; 53 x 35 inches; cotton, lamé, decorative cording and fabric paints; photo by Karen Bell

This quilt is an homage to my birthplace. I was born in Los Angeles, a fourth-generation Californian. Although I left Los Angeles as a young child, I never ceased to be fascinated by the vast expanse of the city. I have always loved to fly into the city at night, when it is so brilliantly lit. The neon lights, the automobile lights, and the street lights make it seem like the city goes on forever. The city is built horizontally, covering all the flat land and crawling up hills. The many miles of streets on the flat are as straight as arrows, while the streets in the mountains curve around the hills and through the passes. Viewed from above, one sees an enormous grid of lights.

To make this quilt I used a small part of a map of Los Angeles to make a pattern for a twelve-inch block. I assembled six blocks from the pattern, altering fabrics and changing some pieces in each block. I then assembled the blocks into the top, adding fabrics and surface details to create the desired effect. The cording is applied over hand-quilted lines. The buildings on the quilt are three-dimensional appliqués.

## METROPOLITAN POSTCARD

Dee Danley-Brown (Westbrook, Connecticut); 1989; 63 x 58 inches; cotton

The desire to make a quilt about New York City had been with me for a long time. I had been collecting fabrics for over a year when the Manhattan Quilter's Guild (of which I am a member) was asked to mount an exhibit of quilts about the city in a gallery in Central Park. By this time I had lived in New York for seven years and had spent a lot of time looking at the architecture of the city. The monumental skyscrapers, the crumbling rows of tenements, the parks, the skyline and the architectural details of unique buildings create a visual dynamic that compelled me to transform the three-dimensional city into a two-dimensional quilt.

I realized that there are many ways to see the city, that to make the quilt with only one view would not be as interesting as looking at it in more than one way. Some of my favorite views are from the high windows of skyscrapers where the perspectives of the city are radically changed from the views at ground level. To see the city from across the river or from Central Park again changes the panorama.

The re-creations of the building did not seem to have to be actual reproductions of them. I tried to capture the essence of special buildings so that some reference was made to them. The triangular design at the top of the quilt represents a very typical decorative element over windows and doorways of small buildings from the late nineteenth century. Such a small decorative detail intrigues me, because it suggests the architect's desire to give each building, no matter how simple, some special detail to make it more appealing.

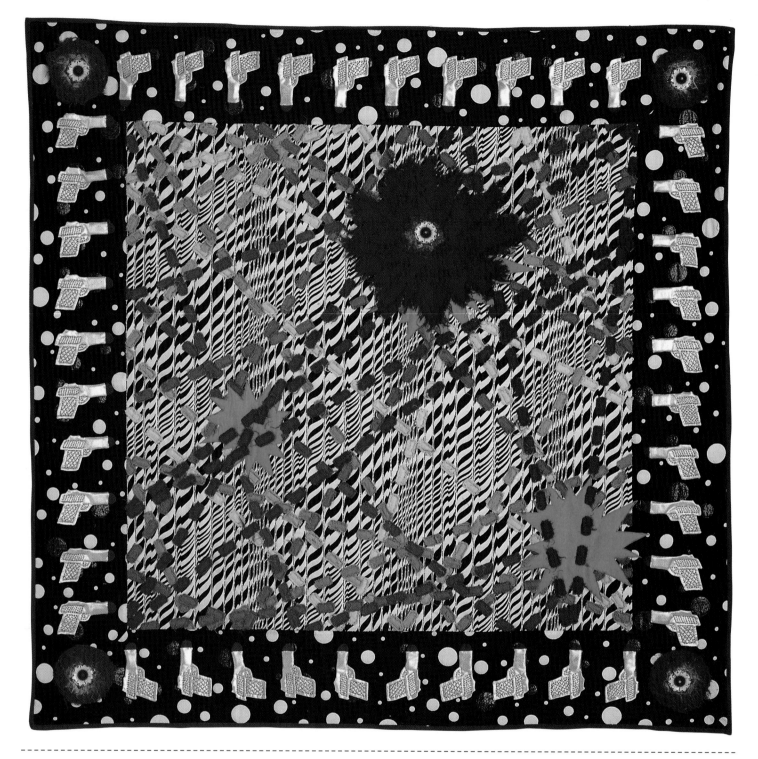

**TARGET...SHE DIDN'T KNOW THE GUN WAS LOADED**

Barbara W. Watler (Hollywood, Florida); 1990; 52 x 52 inches; multi fabrics with mixed media and found objects; photo by Barry Majewski

**W**ords spoken in anger remind me of the old excuse about not knowing the gun was loaded and the tragic harm thoughtlessness can inflict. The quilt graphically depicts the ricochet effect of gun shots. The raveling threads from the trajectory paths of the bullets have been used to create "bullet hole blossoms" in the corners and in the center explosion. With street violence so much a part of my everyday news, the harm of more subtle weapons tends to be forgotten.

**STRUCTURALLY UNSOUND**

Deborah Melton Anderson (Columbus, Ohio); 1990; 56 x 57 1/2 inches; cotton appliqué and reverse appliqué; photo by J. Kevin Fitzsimons

Lazarus Parking Garage #3 was demolished in September 1989 after it was discovered to be "structurally unsound." Sunday afternoons, when the downtown Columbus, Ohio streets were empty and the demolition machinery was motionless, proved to be the best time to record by camera the marvelous patterns created by the twisted structural steel rods and chunks of concrete. The dramatic tangled webs were silhouetted against the cityscape, bathed in the golden afternoon sunlight. We can see the south side of the Lazarus store along with other city and state buildings through the debris.

The demolition site is bordered by elements in the quilt's design. At the bottom, the border recalls the large pieces of plywood, painted black and white, which were used as a barrier. Continuing clockwise, the remains of a concrete pillar and the linear patterned garage ceiling provide borders. The unencumbered view of the city on the right side becomes the fourth border. Imagine the design without it! The viewer would have the sense of being incarcerated, changing the "down but not out" message of the quilt.

Federated Department Stores, including Lazarus, had been taken over by a corporate raider a year or two earlier. The quilt may be understood as a metaphor for the resulting corporate financial chaos, as well as the loss to the public of a favorite institution.

**AFRICAN JAZZ #1**

Michael Cummings (New York, New York); 1990; 72 X 96 inches; cotton

The "African Jazz" series of twelve quilts was developed after I found a black-and-white poster showing three African jazz musicians performing in a smoke-filled room while appearing to be in a hypnotic trance. My thoughts were of a collage of images with references such as Egungun costumes found in the Yoruba society in Western Nigeria, the French painter Rousseau, and Romare Bearden.

It was a challenge to create each one of these large quilts with unique environments for the individual pieces. Intrinsic to my art is an awareness of a cultural heritage that includes ancient histories, non-Western aesthetic formulations and popular art traditions, all coming together to produce my personal expression of an international transcultural aesthetic.

# AFRICAN AMERICAN

The last few years have witnessed a growing appreciation of the African-American aesthetic in contemporary pictorial quilts. Numerous well-received exhibitions, articles, and books have called attention to the story-tellers of African-American life. Artists perpetuate a visual tradition reflecting the events in their lives as well as validating their African heritage and documenting the horrors of slavery and oppression. While African Americans have made quilts in this country since the late eighteenth century, until recently, little was published about their efforts. Noting this change of fortune, Cuesta Benberry, a quilt historian who has chronicled the national expanded consciousness of the African-American aesthetic, predicted in the 1980s that African-American quilts would become "objects of intense interest and scholarly investigations" just as Amish quilts were in the 1970s. With the growth of black studies programs, the women's movement, and state quilt documentation projects, this prediction proved accurate.

Because of the overwhelming response to recent exhibitions including "Always There: The African-American Presence in American Quilts" and "Stitching Memories: African-American Story Quilts" some of the artists in this chapter have become celebrities. Their new works are eagerly awaited by their many fans, including fellow members of the Women of Color Quilters Network, a national organization of over 300 quilters founded by Dr. Carolyn Mazloomi to combat the isolation of black quilters.

Through its newsletter, material of interest is disseminated to the group. In this chapter, Carolyn Mazloomi is represented by two quilts that express the "endurance, suffering, and courage" of her ancestors as well as explore the challenges of today.

Michael Cummings, one of the few male artists in this book, delved into quiltmaking while exploring various aspects of textile art. Totally self-taught, Cummings first made banners and then turned to quilts. For him, being an African American has led to experiencing "an urgent need to address events and issues affecting all people of color." As a boy in L.A., Cummings wanted to be a painter but did not know of any black artists. In years to come in his pictorial quilts, Cummings purposely drew upon African and African-American culture as a source for his work. When Cummings is turned on to a theme, he can't stop with one quilt. After *African Jazz #1* was finished, Cummings spent weekends and evenings completing eleven more versions in a year. Other groups of work including the "Colored Girls" series and the "Haitian Boat People" series reflect his desire to record the international African experience with a bold, colorful palette. Cummings notes, "I credit my strong use of primary color to growing up in L.A., always being in the sun, the colors of the houses, gardens in bloom all year round...."

Yvonne Wells was "discovered" by quilt historian and dealer Robert Cargo in 1981 through a classified ad that read simply: "Quilts for sale, $20 and up. Call after 4 P.M." Wells, an Alabama physical education teacher, had been quilting on her own for two years. Cargo immediately fell in love with her work, believing Wells's quilts "possess that quality to which all artists aspire: they catch the eye and fill us with wonder, delight and at times, awe." Today Wells's work is known throughout the country as museums, galleries and collectors vie for her latest piece. Like many pictorial quilters Wells likes to create an air of mystery, not wanting to force her feelings on the viewer. "I leave lots of space in my art work so people looking can see into it whatever they want. I want people to imagine their own story." Many of Wells's quilts reflect her heritage and address racial injustices. Throughout Wells's work runs a strong spiritual vein, exemplified in recent quilts by the inclusion of little triangles that hold private religious meaning to her.

Always dramatic, always with feeling, all of the African-American quilts in this chapter represent an important contribution to the canvas of pictorial quilting.

**THE MAN—BLACK**

Yvonne Wells (Tuscaloosa, Alabama); 1991; 62 x 80 inches; cottons, wools, polyester blend, corduroys, an Alabama flag, a zipper, and rick-rack; courtesy of the Robert Cargo Folk Art Gallery, Tuscaloosa, Alabama

The Man—Black was returning from the field one day. He had just finished working, and as he was walking home, he put his hoe around his shoulders as he passed a watermelon patch. He saw one that he liked, so he put his foot there as if to mark it and say, "I will come back and get this one later on." You will notice that there are watermelons out in the field, and one had burst (it was a good ripe one). There is also a slice of watermelon on the table with seeds falling on the ground.

The Man—Black, too, was a proud man. He is also wearing a star. There are several stars on this quilt, and these stars are falling on Alabama. This background is mainly the old Alabama flag. This flag was given to me in poor condition, but it didn't matter to me, because I was going to retire it. The Man—Black has a fly sewn onto his trousers. Since this quilt has been made, the question of stereotyping him has been suggested. When I made the quilt, that wasn't my intention. I knew that this man needed a fly in his trousers, so I tore one out of my skirt and put it on him.

**THE MAN—WHITE**

Yvonne Wells (Tuscaloosa, Alabama); 1991; 46 x 79 inches; cottons, upholstery fabrics, corduroys, an American flag, rick-rack, an earring, elastic belt, and a handkerchief; courtesy of the Robert Cargo Folk Art Gallery, Tuscaloosa, Alabama

**A**s he was taking a stroll one day through a garden, these were not flowers he was trampling, but these were the Red man, the Black man, and the Yellow man. He was trampling over these people as if to say, "I am superior." He didn't want to hear their cries, so he took his ears off and placed them underneath a table with a saw buzzing so he wouldn't have to hear them. He has the appearance of a person who is in charge. You will notice he is smoking a pipe and has it clenched in his teeth—maybe he is saying I don't have to listen to anyone; I am the American—even though he is not the true American…. He wasn't all that bad, so I put my belt around him, and anybody who wears anything of mine is not all bad. He has a star on his shoulder—the proud American.

## AN ALBUM OF MEMORIES

Marlene O'Bryant-Seabrook (Charleston, South Carolina); 1990; 85 x 107 inches; cotton; photo by Rich-Steele Pro Labs and Studio

**F**amily and education are important components of my life. This quilt features my high school, the colleges and university from which I received degrees and favorite family photographs which were hand transferred to 100% cotton using laser copies and a commercial transfer medium.

### MA! THE REVEREND JUST ATE THE LAST PIECE OF CHICKEN

Barbara G. Pietila (Baltimore, Maryland); 1992; 34 1/2 x 32 inches;
cotton with glass beads

The church has always been an important institution in the African-American community and remains so to this day. When I was a child, it was considered an honor to have the minister for Sunday dinner. The ladies of the congregation were thus provided with an opportunity to show off their cooking skills and the event became a grand occasion. Fried chicken was a favorite with the best parts reserved for the adults. Some ministers were notorious for their appetites and the cupboard was often bare when the visit was over. One of the elderly ladies in one of my quilt classes told me a story of their minister and how her little brother always broke into tears when the last piece of chicken disappeared. That was the inspiration for this quilt.

### THE WATER BROUGHT US HERE—THE WATER WILL TAKE US BACK

Carolyn L. Mazloomi (Cincinnati, Ohio); 1992; 96 x 108 inches; cottons, beads, mirrors, and shells

Some historians estimate that as many as fifty million people were lost by West Africa as a result of the slave trade that lasted from 1441 until 1850. My ancestors were chained and shackled in the dark holes of ships as they endured the voyage to the West Indies and the Americas. This quilt is a memorial to them—for what they suffered and endured. Many did not survive that voyage and their bodies were simply thrown overboard. Others, when the opportunity arose, threw themselves into the water rather than live without seeing their homeland again. The pools of blood represent those that lost their lives in the Middle Passage.

The triangles are souls in flight—on their way back to the Motherland. On the opposite side of the quilt is a cross symbolizing the Christian faith. Slavers justified their position by claiming to Christianize Blacks, thus showing them the true religion. Spider webs are quilted around this section of the quilt representing traps, for once those that were enslaved left Africa there was no escaping their plight.

Mother Africa and her child watch as her children and relatives are taken from her. This is a testament to my foreparents' endurance, suffering and courage. Analyzing our past helps us to understand the present and gives us strength to continue to exist.

## BEING IN TOTAL CONTROL OF HERSELF

Yvonne Wells (Tuscaloosa, Alabama); 1990; 71 x 81 inches; cotton, cotton blends, and found objects; courtesy of the Robert Cargo Folk Art Gallery, Tuscaloosa, Alabama

This quilt came about as a result of my visit to New York. On the way to New York I noticed the Statue of Liberty. I saw this lady standing very much in control of herself, and I decided to make a quilt with this lady on it.

In the middle of the quilt the lady holds in her left hand a Black man. She has put a piece of tape over the Black man's mouth as if to hush him up…and in her right hand she has money which indicates, "I'm in control because I have the money to buy anything I want. Also, I have the key to unlock anything that may be locked up." Under her feet is an Indian who is the true American, and you notice she has her nails in him and he's crying, saying, "But I am the true American"; but she is in control of everything, so she steps on him and he is unable to speak.

The buildings that you see are those that I saw on Fifth Avenue as I was walking down—Saks and the Trump Tower which was so tall and so gleaming that I thought I'd put it in my quilt. Looking out of the window of my hotel I saw Central Park and its many trees. In this quilt I have made the trees Indians—the true Americans. But this lady who was in control of everything didn't seem to let that bother her.

George Washington, who was the Father of this country, is placed on this quilt beside the symbol of the United States. Above that is the Liberty Bell. Each flag that I use is an old flag—I will not use a new flag simply because to me all flags should have served out their purpose before I'm going to use them in my art. This one was given to me, and I used it.

The smile on this lady's face seems to say I am the only person who is in control. The acronym that is used is "BITCH" and this quilt is therefore called "Being in Total Control of Herself."

**I'LL FLY AWAY**

Michael Cummings (New York, New York); 84 x 84 inches; cottons, fabric paint, beads, buttons, shells; courtesy of Francine Seders Gallery Ltd.

▌wanted to make a visual statement about an era in America's history that focused on slavery, particularly the field worker. The title refers to a gospel song that lifts a person's spirit to freedom and away from burdens and pain.

When making quilts and wall hangings I use the appliqué technique. To sew down the main body of the composition I use a sewing machine. However for the quilting which is very simple, all the sewing is done by hand. I employ some hand embroidery on the surface of the works and add found objects and paint to the surfaces. Most importantly, I then wait for the work to talk to me. It will tell me if it feels completed.

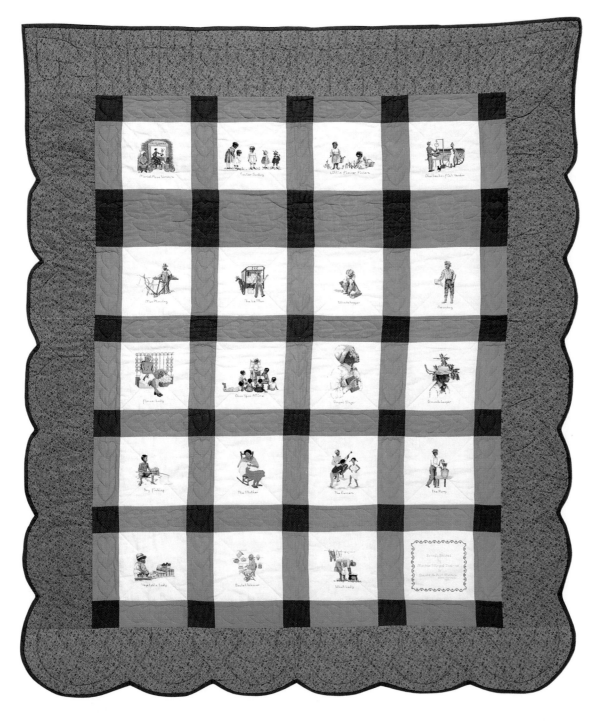

## LOVE, LOVE, LOVE: A RECORD OF A RICH HERITAGE

Marlene O'Bryant-Seabrook (Charleston, South Carolina); 1984; 81 1/2 x 97 inches; cotton; photo by Rich-Steele Pro Labs and Studio

This quilt chronicles childhood recollections based on experiences or observations in and around Charleston, South Carolina. My first intent was to make a "Charleston Quilt," but as I began looking for St. Michael's, the Public Market, The Citadel, the people depicted on the cross-stitch graphs were black. A "Charleston Quilt" viewed by an outsider would strongly suggest that Charleston is a combination of old buildings and black people. Immediately, it occurred to me that I ought to record for my descendants the important contributions made to the city of Charleston by the descendants of slaves. And so my black heritage quilt was born and because it holds very special, personal meanings, I exercised artistic license with the names, colors and skin tones of some of the characters or scenes I selected to portray.

I centered the four scenes that are the epitome of the black experience. "Once Upon a Time" symbolizes the oral nature of a culture noted for the strength of the Mother. When we were "toil-weary," "The Dancers" brought us joy and when we were "heavy-hearted," we turned to the "Gospel Singer" for words of hope.

During the months of cross-stitching, I developed a deep love for the richness of my heritage. To dramatize that love, I quilted many hearts on pink and green, the colors of my sorority, Alpha Kappa Gamma.

**TRYIN' TO GRAB A PIECE OF THE PIE**

Carolyn L. Mazloomi (Cincinnati, Ohio); 70 x 90 inches; hand-painted cottons with beads

Since being brought from the Motherland, we as Black folk have tried to forge a life here in America...and it has never proven to be that easy. Even now there is a lack of full equality, although much of what America is today is a result of the toil of slave labor.

The Black man is shown climbing from his African origins to assimilate into the mainstream of American life. His assimilation has never been quite complete. The money panel represents the good life to be had in this country. The patchwork panel is dedicated to all Black quilters who have contributed so much to the art form in this country.

**THE GOOD SAMARITAN**

Lee Porter (Washington D.C.); 1991; 51 1/2 x 69 inches; cotton and cotton blends; courtesy of Lazarus House, Washington D.C.; photo by Mark Gulezian

**T**he biblical inspiration for this quilt was the story Jesus told in Luke 10: 29–37 about the Samaritan who responded to the needs of the wounded man on the roadside in answer to the lawyer's question about who was his neighbor. The artistic inspiration was a medieval book illustration with a series of meandering lines. I felt that the design framework would allow me to show the number of stages in the Good Samaritan story and to communicate the wounded man's journey from the side of the road to being cared for in the inn.

This piece was made for The Samaritan Inns, a multi-faceted program helping alcoholic and drug addicted people in recovery move from homelessness to self-sufficiency. The quilt hangs in Lazarus House, an eighty-one single-unit housing community for people who are successfully making this journey with Samaritan Inn's support. I feel like a celebrity when I visit Lazarus House for I am known as the "maker of their quilt."

# SPIRITUALITY AND RELIGION

Pictorial quilters pursuing religious subjects view their quilts as symbols of renewal. Since the imagery of renewal and rebirth is at the heart of the Judeo-Christian tradition, this perception is validated by the theology. The soul of their quilts is expressed in visual messages that are either based in theology or spiritual beliefs.

Quilt artists concerned with traditional forms of religion often find inspiration in biblical passages and stories or particular doctrines and tenets of their religions. Artists like Charlotte Anderson, are so well known for their work that they often receive commissions to create quilts reflecting their religious heritage. Charlotte Anderson's latest religious work is a huge quilt commissioned by the Latter-day Saint Museum of Church History and Art, which actively seeks quilts relating to Mormon history. Other artists, including Deborah Anderson, extend their interest to the field of liturgical quilting, creating vestments, altarpieces, torah covers, and banners. Deborah Anderson strives to design works whose complexity will hold the interest of the frequent viewer from many angles and distances.

In contrast, artists Susan Shie and James Acord, evince a strong sense of spirituality in their quilts while eschewing ties to organized religion. Their quilts are rooted in naturalism, New Age teachings, and holistic precepts. Calling their pieces "Healing Quilts," they consider themselves "art shamans." Shie created the "Green Quilts" project in 1989 and since its inception over five hundred quilts have been registered with the organization. Green Quilts aims to foster through quilts the process of bringing the earth back to a balance, back to its perfect state, back, one might say, to a Garden of Eden.

As a group, religious quilts display feelings of serenity and joy. Their makers look to define segments of the Bible that hold particular meaning to them, seek to glorify tenets of their religion, and strive to reveal the beauty of sacred objects and houses of worship. Create a visual narrative or vignette; they richly re-interpret a variety of spiritual themes.

## BASILICA ARMEN-ODZUN

Deborah Melton Anderson (Columbus, Ohio); 1989; 39 x 42 inches; cotton; photo by J. Kevin Fitzsimons

**T**he remains of the Armenian Basilica of Odzun are gray and weathered, yet they still speak of a holy place, a house of worship and prayer. The Byzantine architecture with its multi-windowed dome area, seems to draw an individual into a new state of mind. The Basilica has been given new life through color; the burning votive candles and the floating red carnations (themselves a symbol of life) are arranged to recall the wounds of Christ. I had been studying a black-and-white photograph of Odzun, along with other photographs of Armenia, when the earthquakes of December 1988 occurred. The quilt is dedicated to the victims.

I created *Basilica Armen-Odzun* using machine appliqué and reverse appliqué sewing techniques. I developed my own method of appliquéing fabric to the front by machine stitching on the back of the quilt. I then employed decorative zig-zag stitching by machine to the front of the quilt. I chose colors often found in Turkish oriental rugs, which have been of special interest to me for many years.

## KINGDOMS

Charlotte Warr Anderson (Salt Lake City); 1987; 95 x 85 inches; cottons, silks, 100% polyesters, acetates, rayons, and acrylics; courtesy of the LDS Museum of Church History and Art, Salt Lake City, Utah; photo by Ronald Read

*Kingdoms* was a commission for the LDS Museum of Church History and Art. I submitted three proposals for quilts, and they selected *Kingdoms* because they had no other artwork that depicted this subject matter—the Mormon doctrine of the Three Degrees of Glory. The quilt can be thought of as a family portrait of heaven—everything in its proper order and place after the Millennium and the end of all things (the Dispensation of Heaven).

Most of the quilt is made of a repeated block in the shape of an elongated hexagon to form the rows of people. The Godhead (Father, Son and Holy Ghost) are the three beings at the top of the portrait. Below them are the Three Degrees of Glory in ascending order. The Celestial Kingdom for those who have been good and kind and kept all their covenants is first—the coloring on these beings is more pure and bright. The Terrestrial Kingdom is for those who have been pretty good and benevolent but did not honor all their covenants—more colors have been introduced here. The Telestial Kingdom is lowest and is for your basic person who has committed no terrible sins but has not kept any covenants either. These Degrees of Glory are represented by the glories of the sun, the moon and the stars. The black parts of the quilt represent Hell, Outer Darkness and Perdition. The beings in these sections are incomplete compared to the ones in the Kingdoms. They are true sinners (mass murderers, for example) and are in positions of frustration and despair. At the bottom is a black-on-black star on which stands Satan. He is shaking his fist at God. Even after the Dispensation of All Things he is still defiant.

*Kingdoms* is machine pieced and hand quilted.

## LORD'S PRAYER WITH MARY

Artist Unknown (signed "LZ"); signed 1988; 67 x 75 inches; cottons, synthetic fabrics, human hair, costume jewelry, leather, copper, and tin; collection of Michael J. O'Connell; photograph courtesy of America Hurrah, New York City

**A**lthough this very unusual quilt was found at a tag sale in St. Paul, Minnesota, it was probably originally intended as a gift. Filled with personal and religious messages the quilt focuses on the central figure of a pregnant woman, whose stomach extends an amazing nine inches and appears to be fashioned around a bowl that has been covered with batting and fabric. Supporting characters include figures of a child, an older woman and a loving couple set into a bucolic landscape. A white dove hovers over a gas station—perhaps the workplace of the father. Religious quotes include several from Roman Catholic official texts, the Book of Revelation in the *New Testament*, and *The Lord's Prayer*.

**THE MIRACLE OF THE SEAGULLS**

Marva E. Dalebout (St. George, Utah); 1991; 85 x 85 inches; cotton, cotton blends, lamé, and silk; collection of the LDS Museum of Church History and Art, photo by Ronald Read

In 1848 the Mormon pioneers planted their winter crop of wheat in the Salt Lake Valley. Adversity struck as crickets swarmed down upon the crops, devouring them. The pioneers tried every means to destroy the crickets without success. In final desperation they prayed to the Lord for help. Miraculously, flocks of seagulls descended upon the crickets. The seagulls ate the crickets, then flew away to disgorge in the Great Salt Lake.

The curved patchwork in the wheat and sky are of a scrap-bag variety in blues and golds. Black appliqué silhouettes the seagulls, wheat and crickets. Forty-eight six-inch quilt blocks compose the patchwork border. The black strip borders tell the miracle of this story in cursive quilting stitches that frame the vignette.

### THE WORLD OF THE WONDROUS: A GREEN QUILT

Susan Shie and James Acord (Wooster, Ohio); 1991; 72 x 75 inches; fabric, leather, glass and copper beads, brass, wooden African statues, Bolivian masks, fabric "icicles," crystals and arrowheads; photo by Photography Unlimited

**T**his is a healing quilt commissioned by a family in New York City who feel strong connections to the earth and self-healing. The title, *The World of the Wondrous,* suggests the dimension of the intuitive, unconscious self guided by the Higher Self—the spirit connection to the Divine power. In *The World of the Wondrous* all situations are always perfect. Within the nine-patch design the mother, father and son are shown interacting with nature and involved with various acts of healing. The blessings in this quilt symbolize balancing, safety and peace for all people, animals, plants, rocks, water, winds, etc. The painted, tooled-leather animals are either animals held dear by the son or they are the totem animal spirits of the mother. At the top center of the quilt is a blessing goddess, her arms uplifted as if to say, "Peace to all who live here."

This quilt has a lot of hand sewing in metallic threads, three-dimensional appliqués and masks that can be lifted to reveal faces behind them. It also has its share of machine sewing done on our "fancy Pfaff" which *loves* to write out sentences in rhythmic waves of word-quilting.

**PARABLE OF THE MUSTARD SEED**

Lee Porter (Washington, D.C.); 1991; 26 x 36 inches; cottons; photo by Mark Gulezian

The kingdom of heaven is like a mustard seed which a man took and sowed in his field; it is the smallest of all seeds, but when it has grown it is the greatest of shrubs and becomes a tree, so that the birds of the air come and make nests in its branches. —Matthew 13: 31–32.

I tried to find a picture of the type of mustard plant that Jesus was talking about and could only find a botanical drawing for the Brassica Negra, on which I based this design. I was talking about this with a friend, and she said go out into the country and see the wild mustard blooming. I could picture Jesus sitting on a hillside and telling this parable with the wild mustard surrounding him—it wouldn't have been difficult to understand the power of this tiny seed in that setting.

## BLACK MADONNA: FLIGHT INTO EGYPT

Judith Vierow (Columbus, Ohio); 1988; 35 x 44 inches; cotton, cotton blends, synthetics and buttons; collection of the Liturgical Art Guild of Ohio; photo by Kevin Fitzsimons

The challenge to create this quilt came as I was entering a new phase in my life, artistically and otherwise. The Liturgical Art Guild of Ohio (LAGO) entries were due soon for a show and I had none. However, in meditation I kept seeing the image of a Black woman. Eventually she merged quite naturally with the more traditional Mary, and *Black Madonna* was the result. The guild bought it for their traveling collection.

Since then, I've worked with other images of a Black Goddess; she has become a figure of spiritual transformation affecting all avenues of my life.

## KALEIDOSCOPIC IV: CRYSTAL CANOPY

Designed by Paula Nadelstern (New York, New York) and quilted by Lynn Della Posta; 1989; 74 x 84 inches; cotton and cotton blends; collection of Steven and Michelle Beinhacker, New York, New York; photo by Bobby Hansson

When the mother of the groom commissioned me to make a quilted *chupah*, I immediately connected to her proposal on many levels. A Jewish wedding ceremony takes place under a canopy (a *chupah*) supported by four poles. The custom of using a *chupah* originated with the rabbis in the Middle Ages. Traditionally the wedding ceremony took place outdoors as an omen that the marriage should be blessed with as many children as "the stars of heaven." To separate the ceremony from the marketplace surrounding it, the rabbis sanctioned the use of a *chupah*. The only law governing the size, shape or construction of a *chupah* is that it must be a temporary structure and open-sided.

I welcomed this opportunity to create a beautiful and significant piece of Jewish fold art. What a perfect role for a quilt, typically invested with qualities of comfort and protection! What a natural place to put a fabricated kaleidoscope (my personal quilting mission) right in the middle of a floating, hexagonal Star of David!

The quilt does post-wedding day duty as a bed cover.

**CALLING PLACE**

Erma Martin Yost (Jersey City, New Jersey); 1990; 34 x 30 inches; cyanotype, Mylar, fabric paint, markers and pastels on cotton with Xerox transfers, and machine embroidery

**O**ver the past fifteen years I have spent considerable time seeking out ancient rock paintings left on canyon walls over a thousand years ago by American Indians. One of the most frequent themes in this rock art is the Bighorn sheep. No one knows for certain the purpose of these depictions, but one might guess they were part of a ceremony which petitioned the Spirits for a successful hunt. Perhaps the depictions came in celebration following a successful hunt or were merely a sign to passers-by that this was a habitat of Bighorn. Regardless of the original intent of that prehistoric artist, there is still today a sense of importance, place, and magic when one confronts these rock-art images in their natural setting. These are places that have been frequented by generations, and it is the essence of these sacred sites I have tried to capture.

# N A T I V E  A M E R I C A N

The history of pictorial quilts with Native-American themes began in the early twentieth century when Indian motifs were popularized as design elements, appearing in various magazines and newspapers. Through the popularity of Western movies the public became acquainted with petroglyphs, the drawings of the Ancients on cave walls, sandpaintings, painted hides, and pictorial weavings. Until recently, however, quilts rarely focused on scenes relating to Native-American life.

The name most frequently mentioned in connection with the contemporary scene of pictorial quilts with Native-American themes is Dawn E. Amos of Rapid City, South Dakota. She bases her original designs on Native-American images partly to celebrate the heritage of her husband, who is half Sioux, and partly to explain the meaning of the Native-American experience to her three sons. Her quilts, which have won numerous prizes including the coveted First Place Grand Prize in the 1991 Museum of American Folk Art's "Discover America Contest," have been compared to those of the noted painter James Bama. The drama and environmental realism of her work are heightened by the earthy tones she uses.

Dawn Amos's dignified and powerful designs are matched in the works of other artists in this chapter, including Erma Martin Yost of Jersey City, New Jersey. Yost finds her inspiration in the Indian sacred sites that dot northeast Arizona and southern Utah. In "documenting" the rock-art images of the Anasazi in her work, Yost evokes the natural and spiritual forces that were central to the lives of the Ancients. Descended from a line of Mennonite quilters, Yost combines her quilting heritage with a modern aesthetic, creating assemblages that incorporate cyanotypes, quilt patches, fetish objects, and drawings. The power and the mystery of sacred ceremonies and the magic of the terrain are reflected in works that recognize the harmony of nature. "For me," Yost muses, "there is a visceral recognition of tribal rites. Juxtaposing references to rock art with references to quilt designs may seem incongruent, but both represent things authentic from my past and present experiences."

Fran Soika, an Ohio artist, combined her quilting skills with the traditions of the Acoma Pueblo in New Mexico as represented by the pottery of noted Acoma artist, Drew Lewis. In exchange for some of his pots, Soika executed Lewis's design (after giving him a few hours of quilt design instructions)—and presented him with the finished piece a year later at the New Mexican Quilt Fiesta. This happy collaboration was the result of an extraordinary rapport between two people and two cultures. Other artists have mentioned their fascination and admiration of Native-American life that drew them into a circle of creativity. Marva Dalebout of St. George, Utah, has devoted four quilts to her "Indian Working Women" series while Pat Hill of West Hills, California, has completed a series of "Native-American children." Helen Ocwig's Northwest Coast quilt accurately depicts a ceremonial curtain and is only one of many works featuring motifs from various tribes. All of the artists in this chapter note they have been drawn to these projects by aesthetic interest and a sense of cultural rapport.

There were fewer quilts in this category than in other groups, and one senses that we have seen only the tip of the iceberg. Because of new scholarship, exhibitions and the public's growing appreciation of the Native-American aesthetic, an explosion of new pictorials in this field is a certainty.

## ACOMA QUILT

Quilted by Fran Soika (Novelty, Ohio), designed by Drew Lewis (Acoma Pueblo, New Mexico); 1988; 105 x 73 inches; cotton and cotton blends

The *Acoma Quilt* represents a collaboration with Drew Lewis, a potter from Acoma Pueblo in New Mexico. Drew is from a family of fine potters and travels throughout the country to exhibit his work and teach. The collaboration grew out of a friendship and admiration of each other's skills. Drew's quilt design depicts traditional motifs found on Acoma pottery for centuries. I have lived in the Midwest all my life. New Mexico and its people have introduced me to a different way of life. Visually, the mountains, the mesas, and the desert colors have influenced my work. Spiritually, I have been profoundly affected by the family oriented values of the Native Americans and their sincerity and gentleness.

The *Acoma Quilt* resides at the Acoma Pueblo while a number of hand-coiled pots made from Acoma and Chaco Canyon clay by Drew Lewis are proudly displayed in my home. These works are testaments to the quotation above the entrance to the Museum of International Folk Art in Santa Fe: "The Art of the Craftsman is a Bond Between the Peoples of the World."—*Fran Soika*

**PRAYER FEATHERS**

Erma Martin Yost (Jersey City, New Jersey); 1986; 30 x 28 inches; cotton, colored pencil on rice paper, feathers, and fetish objects

For years my inspiration has come from rock-art images in the American Southwest and alludes to places of prehistoric rituals for power and protection. The Shaman-like figures in *Prayer Feathers* were inspired by a site called the Great Gallery in Barrier Canyon, Utah, where the pictographs are twelve feet tall and date from 0-2000 B.C. As one stands in front of these elaborately painted figures with their bug-eyes and footless bodies, one indeed gets a sense of "Spirits or Deities" that are powerful, larger-than-life, and timeless. It is this sense of sacredness and ceremony I have tried to capture in this work.

**TANNING HIDES**

Marva E. Dalebout (St. George, Utah); 1989; 52 x 60 inches; cottons, cotton blends, and lamé

**T**anning Hides is the fourth quilt I have made in my "Indian Working Women" series. I am inspired by history, then add my imagination when making a quilt. The inside border print provided a beautiful color scheme and gave me an idea for the design that is reproduced in the pink border. The designs employ reverse appliqué in lamé fabric, which is also included in the women's dresses. The warp strings holding the skins on the frame are embroidery floss. The suede cloth for the hide made a perfect animal skin.

**DESCENDING VISIONS**

Dawn E. Amos (Rapid City, South Dakota); 1992; 46 x 62 inches; hand-dyed cotton muslin; photo by Kerdall Remboldt

**B**eing married to a Sioux Indian and raising three sons to be proud of their heritage, I am naturally drawn to deal with the thoughts, emotions, and experiences of Native-American people. However, I like to leave the interpretation of my work to the viewer. I don't want to limit the viewer to my vision.

**RIBBON DRESS**

Pat Hill (West Hills, California); 1991; 43 x 44 inches; cottons, leather, beads, ribbons, and feathers

**R**ibbon Dress is one of a series on Indian children in various settings. The dress is so named because it corresponds with the ribbon shirts the Pueblo men wear. This young maiden was the first subject I integrated with the unique chili pepper designs. The *ristra* (hanging chilis on pueblo walls) is made up of chilis from the same fabric as the border. The feathers are from my daughter's bird, the boots are sheepskin leather, the four pots are from the backing fabric, and the center stone of the necklace is real turquoise. I braided four one-eighth ribbons for the decoration on the dress.

I have always been drawn to Indian designs and culture. I admire their ability to live with the land and use it but not destroy it. The rapport I feel with Native Americans is intriguing, as I am of Norwegian descent.

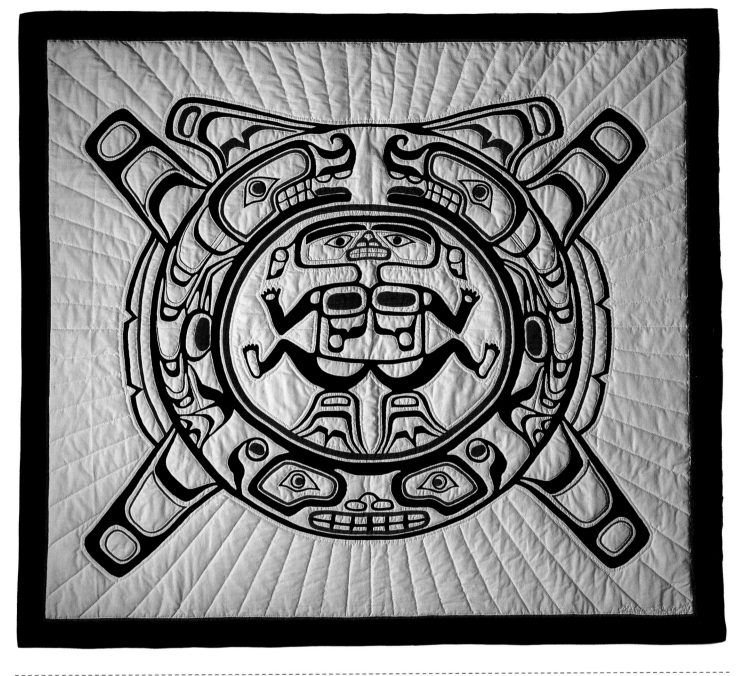

**NORTHWEST COAST INDIAN DESIGN: KWAKIUTL CEREMONIAL CURTAIN**

Helen Ockwig (Yuma, Arizona); 1990; 46 x 50 inches; unbleached muslin, cotton, and cotton blends; photo by Emil Eger

This representation of a Kwakiutl ceremonial curtain from Kingcome Inlet (Museum of Anthropology, University of British Columbia, Vancouver) features both human and *Sisiutl* images. The *Sisiutl* is a mythical creature, usually portrayed as a sea serpent with two heads, which has the ability to change into other forms. When the *Sisiutl* forms a circle, another motif will be in the center—in this case a human being.

I have tried to translate the design as close to the original panel as fabric will allow, using both appliqué and reverse appliqué. I have been fascinated with the idea of transferring to quilt form Indian motifs from many different tribes, including basket and Kachina doll designs. My interest dates back to 1973 when we first visited the Southwest.

**ELVIS**

Yvonne Wells (Tuscaloosa, Alabama); 1991; 81 x 48 inches; cottons, satins, wools, rick-rack, buttons, yarn, and sequins; courtesy of the Robert Cargo Folk Art Gallery, Tuscaloosa, Alabama

**T**his is the second in a series of three Elvis quilts that I have made. Elvis was the king of rock-and-roll. He was very flamboyant in his dress and his action and his movement as he sang and played the guitar. Here, Elvis is wearing one of his shiny suits and a pair of blue shoes. One of his songs was "[Don't Step on my] Blue Suede Shoes." I was unable to find any suede at the time I was making this quilt, so I just used blue. Around his neck he is wearing an Hawaiian lei. One of his movies had an Hawaiian theme. Above his head is a halo because Elvis was considered supernatural, and today there are people who still think he is alive. Notice the big diamond ring that he is wearing on his finger—it's also an indication of his flamboyant nature.

# CELEBRITIES

Artists have always been fascinated with the stars of stage and screen. Radio and television have provided their own celebrities including actors and actresses who also work in theater and the movies. Political figures commanding center stage in our national life and even heroes and heroines of the comics are frequently elevated to celebrity status by artists in various mediums. Quilt artists in particular have been captivated by their favorite luminaries, creating exciting, often amusing, and sometimes poignant works of art.

It is not surprising that the superstars of the moment are most frequently represented in various art forms. Yvonne Wells's series of "Elvis" quilts pays tribute to the man who changed music forever. Her unique perception and treatment captures the allure of the "King," the most popular figure of the 1950s and 1960s. Edward Larson, one of the first pictorial quilt designers to achieve commercial success, also focused on a celebrity, Woody Guthrie, as the subject for a bittersweet "memory" quilt. In his very detailed work, Larson explores the personal unhappiness in Guthrie's life while he celebrates his musical successes.

Among the most successful celebrity quilts are those that depict evocative scenes from a particular era. One quilt by an unknown artist, featuring political and military personalities of the 1950s, provides an interesting historical map of that decade, vividly illustrating people and events that might otherwise be forgotten. In *Salute to Broadway*, a group project, artists pay tribute to their favorite scenes from acclaimed shows. Colorful appliqué blocks give viewers a romantic glimpse of the theater marquee.

Most viewers approach "celebrity" quilts with a set of visual expectations based on their own recollections. Since these quilts exploit a heritage of reminiscence intrinsic to the medium, they always prompt smiles of remembrance.

**FAMOUS AMERICANS**

L. B. Evans ;signed "Cradled in 1951 and 1952"; 61 x 90 inches; cotton; courtesy of America Hurrah, New York, New York

This pieced, appliquéd and embroidered quilt depicts the important military, political, and social figures of the 1940s and 1950s. Each personality is identified with relevant annotations and quotations. Over eighty famous Americans are portrayed, and the list includes: Harry S. Truman, Franklin Delano Roosevelt, Eleanor Roosevelt and Fala, Bess and Margaret Truman, Vice-president Alben Barkley, Dwight D. Eisenhower, Herbert Hoover, Senator Robert Taft, Dean Acheson, Thomas Dewey, John Foster Dulles, J. Edgar Hoover, Harold Stassen, Henry Ford II, Earl Warren, Alger Hiss, Whittaker Chambers, Walter Reuther, Estes Kefauver, Henry Wallace, John L. Lewis, General Douglas MacArthur, General Omar Bradley, General Carl Speatz, General George Marshall, and General Matthew Ridgway.

**FACES**

Sophia Serena Schroeder (Fort Wayne, Indiana); ca. 1950; 53 x 73 inches; linen with embroidery; courtesy of Shelly Zegart, Louisville, Kentucky

The embroidered faces are likenesses of well-known personalities of the 1940s and 1950s, including General Douglas McArthur, Joan Crawford, Bette Davis, Amelia Earhart, Roy Rogers and Dale Evans, Imelda Marcos, President Sukarno, and Leopold Stokowski. The artist sewed a pink sunbonnet to represent herself adorned with her initials, "S.S."

**COMIC STRIP**

Anonymous; ca. 1960s; cotton; courtesy of Susan Parrish Antiques, New York, New York

Everybody's favorite characters from the comics—from Nancy to Little Lulu to Daffy Duck—is featured on what probably was intended as a child's bedcover judging from the scalloped edges of the border. The figures must have been traced from the actual comics, as the likenesses are completely accurate.

**MICKEY AND MINNIE**

Anonymous; dated January 16, 1936; 78 x 60 inches; cotton; courtesy of American Hurrah, New York City

**M**ickey and Minnie are among Walt Disney's most famous animated figures. They are thought of as icons of American pop culture and have been frequently depicted on quilts.

**WOODY GUTHRIE**

Designed by Edward Larson (Santa Fe, New Mexico), quilted by Alice Dunsdon (Glenwood, Iowa); 1987; 120 x 96 inches; cotton

I design quilts as if I am telling a story; I try to highlight events to give them emotional emphasis visually. In the corner of this piece I put Woody's two heroes—Will Rogers and Jesus Christ. Throughout the quilt I depicted the joys and tragedies that composed Woody's life, such as his illness, Huntington's chorea, a hereditary disease.

Woody grew up not far from where I did. He is about fifteen years younger than I am—so I was a kid while he was a young man during the Great Depression. I know very little about his experiences, but I admire his tenacity in the face of all odds and his joy as expressed through his songs that encouraged a whole group of discouraged folks.

The factory depicted on the quilt celebrates the populist, Joe Hill. Woody loved the working people and the hoboes, who like him, rode the rails; so I placed him standing on a train track. The sign, "Rt. 66"—the mother road—refers to Woody's favorite song, "This Land is Your Land." Other scenes reflect the deaths of his sister and daughter, the fire that destroyed his house, and the success of Woody's son, Arlo, who composed "Alice's Restaurant."

Alice Dunsdon followed my pattern (a one-to-one drawing of the quilt and a sketch done in Crayolas with the colors I chose). Crayolas are kind of indefinite. They are a means I've found to deepen the involvement of the quilter, who has to interpret and bring to the work personal ideas about color and fabric. This makes the quilt more of a collaboration—a shared work of the quilter's aesthetics and my drawing.—*Edward Larson*

## SALUTE TO BROADWAY

Needles End Quilting Group, directed and quilted by Lupe Miller (New York, New York); 1985; 90 x 90 inches; cotton, cotton blends satin, silk, fur, metallics and wool; collection of the Museum of American Folk Art

**T**hirty urban quilters re-create the best of Broadway from *South Pacific* and *The King and I* to *My Fair Lady* and *Hello Dolly* in sixteen panels glorifying the theater. Their lively depictions depend on soft sculpture and lustrous fabrics to re-enact scenes containing details taken straight from the various shows: Henry Higgins spots a real cashmere sweater, Carol Channing preens in fuchsia plumage, and the *Fiddler on the Roof* wedding guests wear pure silk black coats.

**GOODBYE CRUEL WORLD . . . I'M OFF TO JOIN THE CIRCUS**

Emily Owens (Pacific Grove, California); 1991; 51 x 71 inches; cotton, cotton blends, beads, Xerox transfer, and plastic army soldiers and camels; photo by Christopher Hulse

I made this quilt during the Gulf War. It reflects the folly of all wars and specifically the devastating effect on the environment. I made it to relieve "CNN stress." It is a view of the war from the camel's perspective. My quilt was hand appliquéd, hand quilted, and it includes a Xerox transfer to create the camel.

# POLITICAL STATEMENTS

Stenciled hand grenades, machine guns, and propaganda posters are scarcely the first images that come to mind in word associations with quilts, but they and other power symbols are increasingly seen in the quilts of artists making serious political statements. Nancy Erickson's works "are generally about the humor and tenacity involved in communities of individuals during times of chaos, disintegration, and fragmentation." Quilters such as Katherine Knauer delight in creating juxtapositions of disquieting imagery in a medium that is often associated with comfort and safety. Knauer wants her work to "make people stop and think" and believes her quilts to be "a resonance of images in my life and the world in general."

Dissatisfaction with the state of the world and disaffection for political dogma expressed through the eye of the needle have held an enduring place in American quilting. At the other end of the spectrum manifestations of patriotism have also found a home in the American pictorial quilt. From the first "eagle" quilts celebrating the birth of the nation, to the "coffin" quilts mourning soldiers' deaths in the Civil War and the popular portrait quilts of political figures, pictorial quilts have made strong statements on the burning issues of each era.

Today trends in political quilts closely mirror current events. Desert Storm inspired many quilts as artist, Nancy Erickson notes while "CNN went on and on." The horror of oil-slickened animals, the specter of nuclear bombardment and the excesses of propaganda were some of the war-related topics that concerned pictorial quilters. On the domestic front, Sue Pierce explores homelessness in our society in her innovative quilt *When the Safety Net Fails,* and Merrill Mason takes on the industrial landscape of a shipyard with a series of quilts.

In a more optimistic vein other artists, including Yvonne Porcella and Helen Cargo, choose to emphasize the joys of living in America. In the late 1980s and 1990s quilt competitions organized by the Museum of American Folk Art for two of the Great American Quilt Festivals, "Expressions of Liberty" and "Discover America and Friends Sharing America," induced quilters throughout the country and abroad to create an intriguing assortment of variations on a patriotic theme. These statements about what America means to each of the artists provide a quilt textbook of special remembrances, discoveries, and poignant reflections.

The trend toward political pictorial quilts continues to soar, as more quilters employ their needles to assess domestic policy and world events. Some artists incorporate slogans and symbols of political campaigns into quilts, emphasizing the message with sewn-on political buttons, ribbons and other campaign mementos. Other artists work solely in cloth, relying on color and form to express their feelings. As a group, political quilts are among the loveliest, reflecting the passion of artists who can barely contain their deeply felt beliefs.

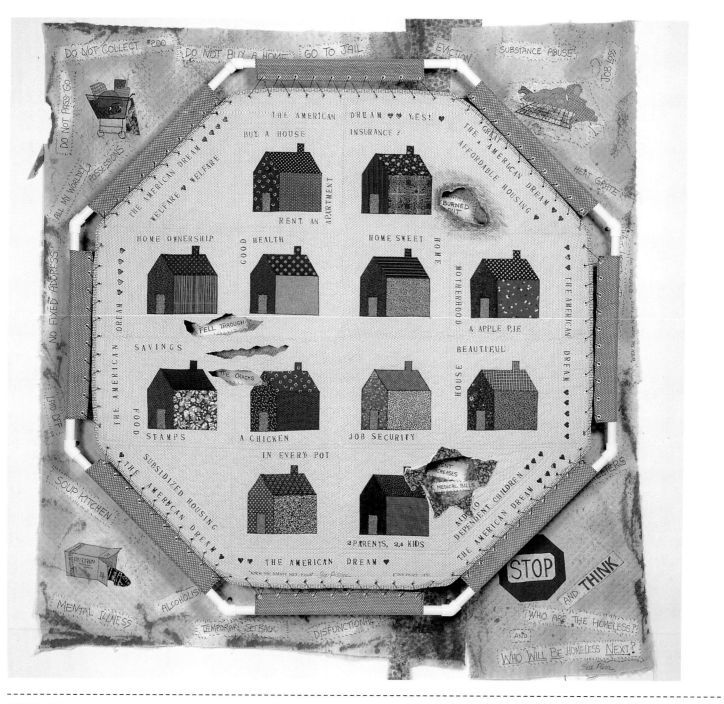

**WHEN THE SAFETY NET FAILS**

Sue Pierce (Rockville, Maryland); 1991; 78 x 72 inches; cotton, cotton blends, textile paints, embroidery thread and a PVC pipe

This piece deals with the important role that shelter plays in our lives. Quilting serves well to portray the red, white, and blue American dream of neat little houses all in a row and the warm feeling of having a place to call home. Because neatness and perfection are so much the expected standard, this medium is also an effective way to draw attention to the jarring reality of jagged holes in the social system which people do indeed fall through. The partially hidden layer of homelessness has no appliquéd houses or embellishment, only the catch phrases that are associated with people who live in the streets: "Fell Through the Cracks," "No Fixed Address," etc. This, too, is a quilt and one that might even provide comfort to someone huddled on a heating grate.

The multiple-layer installation includes a background quilt which hangs directly on the wall and contains phrases and imagery related to homelessness. The front layer is the "safety net" of the title, a quilt tightly stretched on an octagonal frame of PVC pipe. Hidden legs of clear plexiglass keep this section six inches away from the wall when it is hung over the background quilts. This more visible quilt represents the American Dream with neat rows of homes portrayed in red, white, and blue. Rubber-stamped words and phrases list myths, clichés, and social services that are designed to help people hang on to those hopes even during tough times: "Home Sweet Home," "The American Dream," etc. But this safety net doesn't save everyone; there are holes in the quilt, cut and burned, which reveal the darker truths for those without homes.

**MINEFIELD**

Judy Becker (Blaine, Washington); 1991; 61 x 42 inches: cotton; photo by David Caras

**M** *inefield* is a political quilt, made during the Gulf War. The columns of a ruined temple represent a great culture that has survived for centuries. The minefield symbolizes the assault on all civilization that war brings and my sorrow that we have not learned more from the past.

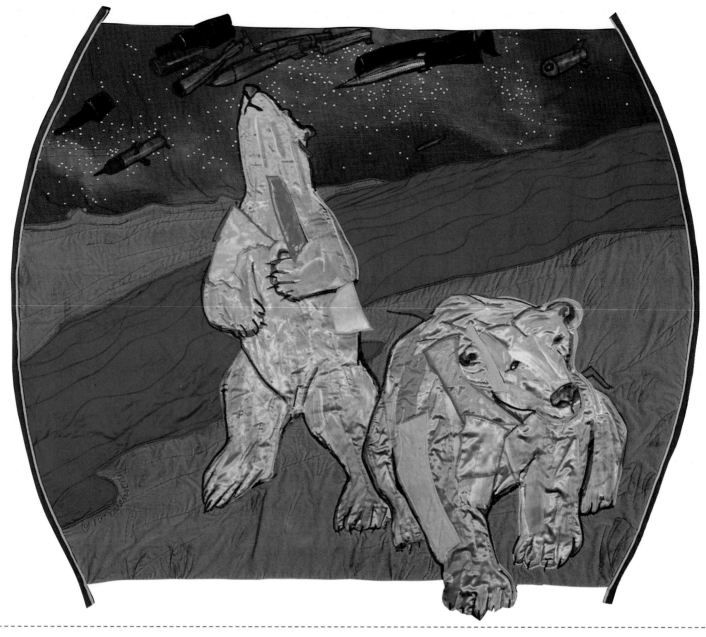

**AURORA HORRIBILIS**

Nancy N. Erickson (Missoula, Montana); 1991; 68 x 57 inches; velvet, cotton, satin and paint; photo by Nancy N. Erickson

**A**urora Horribilis is part of an ongoing series of works about the disconnectedness of humans with other people, other animals and the land. The piece evolved along with the latest war, but it was especially made for the Sacred Bear exhibition (organized by the Missoula Museum of the Arts), though there is nothing sacred about the events which transpired during its construction. The tone of the piece changed constantly; I now see that it is related specifically to that oil-covered cormorant, wonderingly trying to groom itself, on a slippery rock in the blackened Gulf Sea. This tone was not intentional, it merely happened, as CNN went on and on.

Formally, I am experimenting with different modes of containing the pieces, and in this case two curved "frames" are used. As far as specific techniques, I make a drawing, then enlarge the drawing and transfer it to the appropriate fabric. All the pieces are pinned to the background fabric and filler material, rearranged, glued, and appliquéd together. The back side of the piece, often cotton or velvet, is tacked on by hand. Velcro is used for attaching the piece to the wall.

**PROPAGANDA POSTERS**

Katherine Knauer (New York, New York); 1991; 65 x 65 inches; airbrushed and pieced cottons; photo by Myron Miller

**A** variety of world events in 1990 and 1991 inspired this quilt. The fall of communism, *perestroika* and *glasnost* brought long-excluded Soviet art to our country, including a retrospective of the work of Kasimir Malevich at the Metropolitan Museum of Art. Suddenly Soviet art was available in auctions and galleries.

In this quilt I have adapted a traditional quilt pattern, "Feathered Star," to a five-pointed flag design. In the spaces created by the arms of the star I appropriated World War I political images from Malevich's folk-style Russian-government-sponsored broadsheets (small posters that were as common in 1914 as message tee-shirts are today). The broadsheets functioned the same way all propaganda functions: to make the home forces appear invincible and heroic while the enemy appears incompetent, evil, and ridiculous (note Malevich's idiotic, obese German general about to send his troops into a swamp in the lower center section).

Working on this quilt while the television (tuned to CNN) went on and on about Operation Desert Storm, I couldn't help but wonder if some comparisons could be made. Substituting the Soviet flag for the ubiquitous Stars and Stripes of American patriotic quilts, this work becomes a warning against being sucked unnecessarily into a war machine by the passions of the times.

## BOYS WILL BE BOYS

Katherine Knauer (New York, New York); 1987; 79 x 75 inches; stenciled and pieced cottons; photo by Schecter Lee

**B**oys *Will Be Boys* is a general musing on the effect of testosterone on human history, and was probably inspired by an afternoon of watching my two young sons scrapping with each other. Scenes from six separate wars—prehistoric, the Crusades, the American Revolution, World War I, Vietnam and present/future—were first hand-stenciled onto off-white cotton squares. Another original fabric print—red rats on a yellow background—represents both the rodent and human species of rat who become fat during time of war. The border print fabric of the "Little Guy"—portraying the taxpayer with a huge burden to shoulder—climbs up each side. Commercially printed camouflage fabric finishes the quilt top.

## STATUE OF LIBERTY II

Helen Cargo (Tuscaloosa, Alabama); 1987; 42 x 52 inches; cotton

In 1986 my first *Statue of Liberty* was the Alabama winner in the Great American Quilt Contest sponsored by the Museum of American Folk Art to celebrate the centennial of that monument. That quilt showed Native Americans welcoming ethnic groups from around the world with the Statue of Liberty proclaiming their unqualified welcome in the words of Emma Lazarus. As soon as I finished the quilt, I immediately embarked upon *Statue of Liberty II*. I wanted to update the symbolism and depict the scene a hundred years later—in the present.

In this version Americans (red, yellow, black, and white) are still drawn to the statue but now as citizens and tourists. The photographs they are taking are represented by the four slides (still in a film strip) which were required for entering the contest. The gift of the statue to the United States by the French government to acknowledge our common commitment is represented by the flags used as corner blocks and the words, "France—Liberty—America" quilted into the wide borders.

The same cotton fabrics are used in both quilts, and the picture is rendered in appliqué and reverse appliqué in the film's edge.

### SHIP SHAPE

Merrill Mason (Jersey City, New Jersey); 1991; 89 x 80 inches; phototransfers on cloth with embroidery

**M**y work combines photography with the traditional women's art form of quiltmaking and embroidery, aiming to create lush, seductive images out of the industrial landscape. Recently I have concentrated on photographing a toxic chromium waste dump and a scrap-metal site, both in my neighborhood. For this work I zeroed in on the relics of a shipyard containing what were once giant merchant-marine ships. The photographs are transferred to fabric and assembled in a grid, recalling an elemental quilt format. The overall image is then manipulated with appliqué, embroidery and quilting, partially obscuring the grid. The objects in the photographs become identifiable only on close inspection. Stitching, whether by hand or machine, acts as a gestural drawing in addition to providing texture and structure.

I want my work to reflect and illuminate the times and the world I live in. I use my quilts to consider social and political issues by contrasting the conventional associations of the medium (beauty, security and domesticity) with unlikely provocative content, and by treating ugliness as though it were beautiful. I also look to challenge preconceptions about traditional art forms and their capacity for universal artistic expression.

**I LOVE AMERICA**

Yvonne Porcella (Modesto, California); 1989; 70 x 50 inches; cottons; courtesy of Cornell Gallery, Atlanta, Georgia; photo by Sharon Risedorph

America is such a great country, the land of opportunity and invention. We live a fast-paced lifestyle where everything is quick and easy. Our lives are compressed into the fifteen-minute television spot. Even the beautiful word "love" has been reduced to the commercial icon of a red heart.

It seemed appropriate to enshrine the famous red heart in my quilt, *I Love America* by placing the heart on a field of stars and stripes and surrounding it with floating roses and vases of flowers. Inside the heart are symbols of what America loves. The heaven-on-earth layer of the quilt portrays a higher level of iconography found only when traveling through those golden gates.

**THE RED HOUSECOAT: A SELF PORTRAIT**

Carol Ann Wadley (Hillsboro, Oregon); 1990; 62 x 58 inches; cotton and cotton blends, bridal veil, fabric paint, and sequins; photo by Bill Bachhuber

This quilt was designed in a workshop given by Deborah Felix. We were to take fabrics that meant something to us and a small photo of ourselves. I chose fabrics given to me by my mother, friends, and fabrics I did not like or were left over from other projects and other classes. The first top was too small and not pleasing to me, and so I scrapped it and started all over with this one.

I had fallen asleep on the couch with my cats after insisting that I get to watch the program of my choice that night instead of the nightly sports. I fell asleep before the first commercial, and my husband took this picture to prove to me that I too, slept in front of the TV (one of my pet peeves when *he* did it).

The quilt is embellished with stenciled butterflies. I made the butterfly stencil from a potato and used blue fabric paint. I was originally only going to stencil the butterflies on the wallpaper but enjoyed the process so much I put them everywhere. They are to remind me of my very happy childhood, and later I was told the butterflies are symbolic of emerging—which I am—from quilter to artist, from wife to widow to independent woman.

# WOMEN'S CONCERNS

One of the women's movement's greatest contributions to the history of quilting has been to focus attention on the role that quilts have played in women's lives. By doing so the movement set the stage for the new respect accorded to pictorial quilts and slowly convinced a sometimes grudging art world to look at these quilts in a new light. This is not to say that all artists whose quilts merit being placed in this chapter consider themselves part of an organized movement or even that they would be comfortable calling themselves feminists. Their quilts, however, express sentiments that concern women today and are representative of problems that trouble women in all parts of the country.

Many artists dealing with women's issues speak of the fascination of expressing unorthodox ideas in a conventional framework. Cherry Partee in her statement about her quilt, *Green Coverlet*, examines the ramifications of "violating" the traditionally soft surface of what is generally regarded as a woman's medium with violence both in technique and content. The element of surprise works very well in quilts such as Partee's and forces the viewer to take a second look. It can be said that the women's movement has freed artists who wish to break away from traditional subjects and deal with topics that in the past were either forbidden or not fully conceptualized.

One of these formerly taboo subjects, divorce, is both humorously and agonizingly chronicled by two artists in this chapter—Katharine Brainard and Terrie Mangat. Brainard's *Divorce Quilt* has received a great deal of attention in the media. It was featured in *People* magazine. Most of the quilt was sewn as a form of therapy during two exhausting weeks before the end of her ten-year marriage. Terrie Mangat's quilt, *Cash Flow*, was conceived after her divorce settlement and is also an attempt to deal with the bitterness of divorce. Both quilts alleviate pain with infectious humor. If there is a common thread in the quilts of this section, it is the imaginative humor that courses through the work. One of the most amusing pieces is *They're All Alike in the Dark* by Barbara Watler, who imbues her mailboxes with anthropomorphic wit.

Quilts in "*Women's Concerns*" also deal with the more positive aspects of change: hope and growth. Terrie Mangat's other quilt in this section, *Sanctos Sisters Sorority #2*, celebrates women's support groups and in a reflective self-portrait, *The Red Housecoat*, Carol Ann Wadley includes butterflies as symbols of emerging "from quilter to artist, from wife to widow to independent woman."

Whatever the sentiments expressed, whatever the points of view, quilts from the women's camp are electrifying in content and style.

**CASH FLOW**

Terrie Hancock Mangat (Cincinnati, Ohio); 1990; 112 x 118 inches; oil on canvas, fabric and mixed media

**C**ash Flow is a depiction of the marital material garden. It is about the separation of marital assets in the settlement of my divorce. The fence around the garden is made of the sixty pieces of Bucalati silverware. I found that it was easier to return this silver to my husband after I painted each piece in oil on canvas. As I painted the picture, I could see my reflection in the bowls of the spoons and on the blades of the knives. There is a gold ribbon connecting the silver fenceposts. Hidden in the gold are segments of barbed wire. Stitched in as the rows of the garden, my own fur coat stands to remind the viewer that I will not be stepping out in that style in the future. The embroidered flower which has escaped into the sky represents me. Also in the sky, the yellow ribbon represents hope and the eyeballs represent wisdom.

**THEY'RE ALL ALIKE IN THE DARK**

Barbara W. Watler (Hollywood, Florida); 1986; 52 x 30 inches; colored pencil on mixed fabrics; photo by Anne Andrews

The title of this quilt refers to a particularly obnoxious male chauvinistic phrase often used by young men in my era. My observation is that in these enlightened days of feminine freedom, turnabout is fair play and just about as accurate.

*They're All Alike in the Dark* is one of the continuing series of mailbox quilts painted with colored pencils on fabrics. Thus far they number only six, but I have a large collection of photographs and sketches from the past several years. I really enjoy searching out the unusual and remarkable variety of mailboxes. Painting with colored pencil on fabrics is a challenging medium, and I take much pleasure in the feel of pencil on paper. I have a theory that mailboxes are in a way mini portraits of the households they represent. For me they tend to take on anthropomorphic qualities.

**DIVORCE QUILT**

Katharine Brainard (Rockville, Maryland); 1990; 72 x 108 inches; 100% cottons, poly-cottons, beads, buttons, ribbons, acrylic fur, acrylic paint

**T**he *Divorce Quilt* was cathartic—a way of dealing with the bitterness of divorce. I knew I had all this energy about the divorce and I didn't want it inside of me, keeping it there, because it gets toxic. So I took it out of me and put it into the quilt.

A central panel tells the story in tiny embroidered red letters:

My husband bought himself a Mercedes. My husband bought himself a boat. He spent weekends on the boat "alone." "It's so relaxing," he said. One Friday night, I packed milk and cookies and took the kids out to a marina for a bedtime snack with Daddy. We found Daddy naked with a 23-year-old secretary from Daddy's office.

"THIS IS MY BOAT," he yelled. "And what I do on MY BOAT is MINE!!"

**O**ne of the fifteen panels displays a voodoo doll of Brainard's ex-husband (portrayed as balding) with hatpins stuck in strategic body parts, while another portrays him as a snake in the grass. A horrifying block has frogs, bats and insects spewing out of a frightening face over which a sign proclaims, "he lies." For another block Brainard painted a tire of her station wagon and drove over a fuzzy cat cut-out representing her rival whose name was Kitty. Another panel titled "A Happy Thought," reads "Once upon a time, there was a man who lied. So his most prized possession turned black and fell off…" A panel depicting a pair of feet with pretty painted toenails refers to a comment by her husband. "I was making a quilt and my husband came into the room and said, 'God, your feet really look old,' and walked out. I remember looking down at my feet and thinking, 'Huh? Compared to whose?' Boy, nothing clicked." In a quilt whose borders contain a sewn-on broken strand of pearls and little white satin wedding dress buttons, the sentiments expressed reflect a trail of tears and broken promises—a betrayal of the American Dream.

**PANDORA'S BOX**

Katherine Knauer (New York, New York); 1986; 57 x 59 inches; stenciled cottons, plastic spiders, pearls and "gems"; photo by Karen Bell

**P**andora's Box contemplates the Greek myth of the woman who went mad taking the blame for everyone else's problems. The stenciled border design of grasping monster hands mirrors her insanity and proclaims her terror. It was inspired by a story told by a friend: as a child living in India, her bright red hair made her so attractive that people felt compelled to try and touch her, causing her nightmares which lasted for years. The four corners squares in the Crazy Quilt pattern are a gentle pun on their name. The quilt was a technical exercise for myself in printing a light color over a dark printed fabric, and also uses quite a bit of embellishment.

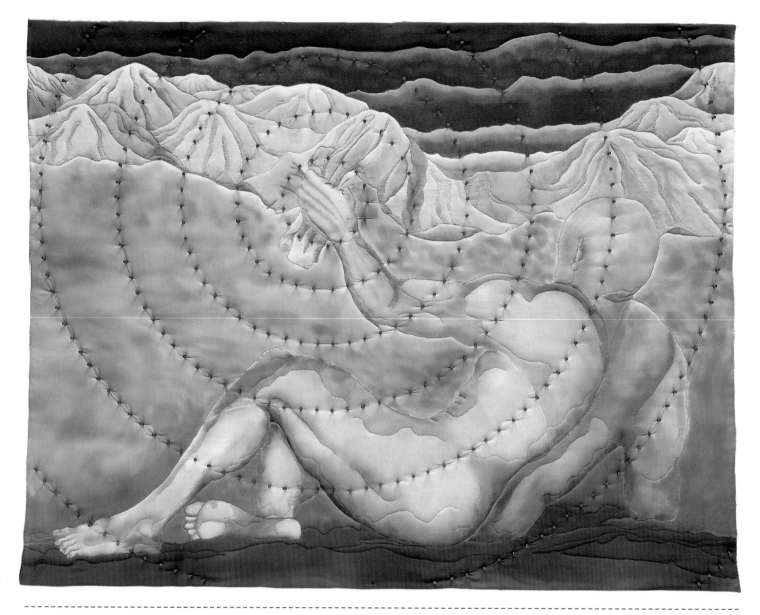

**GREEN COVERLET**

Cherry Partee (Edmonds, Washington); 54 x 68 inches; wood pulp, rayon, and rusted concrete nails; photo by Grover Partee

When I began this work, I had been thinking about simple role reversals and how such a visual presentation can help us think about a problem in a new way. When I showed this quilt to friends, one of the first questions asked was, "Whatever happened to Mother Nature?" Questions I had hoped to raise are: What happens when only one gender is seen as part of nature? Who is it that is targeting nature for destruction, and is it really "Nature" that is being targeted? What does it mean to violate a soft quilt surface, traditionally a woman's medium, with artifacts of a traditionally male medium? What does it mean for a female quiltmaker to do this?

*Green Coverlet* was hand dye-painted using a presist resist and hand quilted. I covered a plywood backing with muslin and attached the quilt with hand stitching to the frame. The rusted concrete nails were hammered in "violating the soft quilt surface."

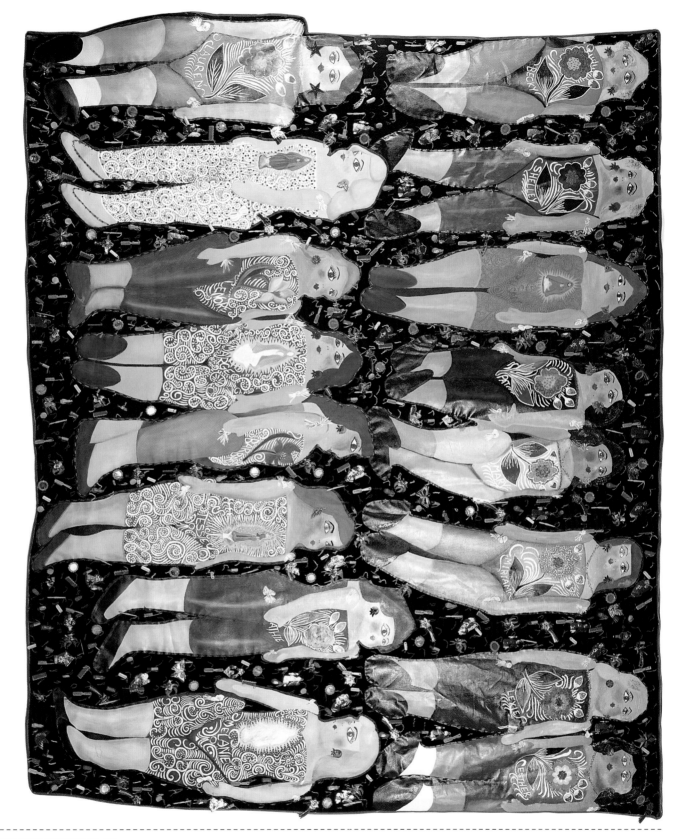

## SANCTOS SISTERS SORORITY #2

Terrie Hancock Mangat (Cincinnati, Ohio); 1990; 55 x 85 inches; oil on canvas, embroidery thread, fabric, and plastic trinkets

The Sanctos Sisters quilts are about women's support groups. In the first one I named the dolls all of the names of my friends and sisters, grandmother, mother, and daughter—all of whom supported me through rough times. In this second quilt I named the dolls after those who have been supportive to me in my quiltmaking career. All are women except Josephine, who is really named after my brother, Joe. Joe has been a great help and was pouting about not having been given recognition.

### AM I DREAMING?

Leslie Hatch-Wong (San Francisco, California); 1990; 54 x 60 inches; cotton and rubber stamped fabric; photo by Sharon Risedorph

The Loma Prieta earthquake occurred in San Francisco just after five o'clock one afternoon in 1989. The shaking and destruction was so frightening that it inspired me to make a quilt to show how I felt on a day that changed history and our lives.

To make the quilt, I first thought carefully about my reactions to the quake. I remembered that I was in a dream state for days after the event, and I wanted this to be the main focus of the quilt. I also remember many of my thoughts running through my mind like a typewriter. The day of the earthquake was strangely warm and windless. I remember many dogs barking outside, and this gave me the idea for the borders of the quilt. In our apartment broken dishes were scattered everywhere across our floors, so I rubber stamped dishes flying through the air on the quilt. After finishing this "storybook" quilt, I realized it helped me feel and release many of the emotions I had about the earthquake.

*Am I Dreaming?* is machine pieced, hand appliquéd, and hand and machine quilted.

# NATURAL WONDERS

It is not surprising that artists intrigued with the process of "creating" should be fascinated by the wonders of the universe. Here, artists marvel at nature's beauty and tranquillity, reflect upon the sun, moon and the stars or are struck by the forces nature unleashes.

In 1989, the Loma Prieta earthquake occurred, causing devastation unparalleled since the major earthquake of 1906. Leslie Hatch-Wong and Deanna Davis were only a few of many pictorial quilters who responded to this tragedy by working through their fears creatively. Although less spectacular than the earthquake, the storms of the North Sea coasts inspired Liese Bronfenbrenner to portray a raging sea- and windswept beaches in her *Storm-Windmills*. Like many quilt artists who wish to capture a moment in time, she relied on personal sketches and photographs, returning again and again to the path of the storm.

While the landscapes of these quilts are real, they are empowered by the artists' emotions and are distilled by their personal recollections and visions of the scene or "event." Some can be seen as metaphors for physical and emotional turmoil while others reflect the passage of time and richness of life.

**STORM-WINDMILLS**

Liese Bronfenbrenner (Ithaca, New York); 1992; 46 x 39 inches; cotton, acrylic and fabric paint, and transfer crayons

I have always loved the sea, especially in windy and stormy weather. Last fall I spent a week on an island off the North Sea Coast, and there I experienced a wild and powerful storm with wind, hail and surging tides. The rapidly moving and ever-changing cloud formations were extraordinary. When I returned to the hotel after one walk, I mentioned to one of the hotel employees that the cloud colors in the skies of the local painters were very real and not just abstract interpretations. The woman answered, "You mean all that gray?" To make sure that I had not just imagined the colors and force of the storm, I made some color sketches and took photographs of the view from my window of the sea, the oncoming storm clouds, the flat fields with the wind bent trees and the loneliness of starkly white windmills on the dikes.

While I was still on the island, I decided to make a wall-quilt of the storm and the windmills. On my return home I began the project by painting cotton drill with acrylic and fabric paints. Then I cut up the painted fabric and joined the pieces to create a design based on my sketches and photographs as well as my memories of the storm. I added additional color to some of the patches with transfer dye crayons and stencils. Some of the patches were joined and the outside edges bound with narrow strips of printed cotton fabrics. Machine and hand embroidery, the latter with silk thread, was used throughout the piece, which was hand quilted. All in all not only was this a good project, but it also represented a satisfying experience that brought back memories of an exhilarating, unforgettable week.

## SKY/SAND/SEA

Linda Levin (Wayland, Massachusetts); 1990; 35 x 51 inches; Procian dyed cotton on canvas backing

I'm interested in exploring the balance between complex patterns and strong, clear structural elements in composition. *Sky/Sand/Sea* is an effort to deal with this problem in the question of landscape—specifically beach, sea, and a vast expanse of sky. The quilt is built directly on a backing of canvas with sewn-on, hand-dyed fabrics. The raw edges are purposely exposed to give a spontaneous, direct, painterly feeling. It is my hope that my work can approach painting while retaining the tactile qualities of fiber art.

## KALEIDOSCOPIC VIII: THE SUN, THE MOON, AND THE STARS

Paula Nadelstern (New York, New York); 1991; 94 x 60 inches; cottons and cotton blends

I am intrigued by the structure of fabricated kaleidoscopes...by the mechanical skill involved in the intricate piecework combined with the challenge of finding the relationships between fabrics. I try to free myself from a conventional sense of fabric orderliness, and seek a random quality to imitate the succession of chance interlinkings synonymous with kaleidoscopes.

Depending on the placement of color, and the resulting degree of contrast, different shapes are emphasized and visually linked. The symmetrical repetition of the design, inherent in the kaleidoscope configuration, creates a visual pattern of inferred lines. Some patches connect to their mirror images and act as if reflected so that a plethora of new symmetrical patterns are created, and the whole becomes greater than its parts.

I have made eight quilts in the kaleidoscope series; already numbers nine and ten are twinkles in this maker's eye.

## JOY IN THE JOURNEY

Carol Johnson (Nibley, Utah); 44 1/4" x 52 1/4"; cotton, metallic fabric and synthetics; 1990

*Joy in the Journey* is the third work in a series of three quilts I have made from pictures I took of the Grand Canyon. I wanted to depict the feelings I had experienced when rafting in this part of the Grand Canyon surrounded by massive green rock and deep green water. Each bend in the river brought different colored rock and water. When we would ask the head boatman what was next, he would say, "Have joy in the journey." Thus the title was born.

The scripture, from the Mormon *Doctrine and Covenants* 128:23 "Let the mountains shout for joy and all ye valleys cry aloud; and ye seas and dry lands tell the wonders of your Eternal King! and ye rivers, and brooks, and rills, flow down with gladness," also mirrors my feelings about this awesome part of nature. I am concerned about the conservation of our natural resources and preservation of the integrity of Grand Canyon National Park. *Joy in the Journey* turned out to be a personal favorite of mine, because it captures a scene of peaceful serenity and reflects my love of the outdoors.

The quilt is machine pieced, employing various strip pieced techniques. It is hand and machine quilted. When the work was finished, it seemed to say, "frame me"—so it is in a simple silver frame rather than a traditional binding.

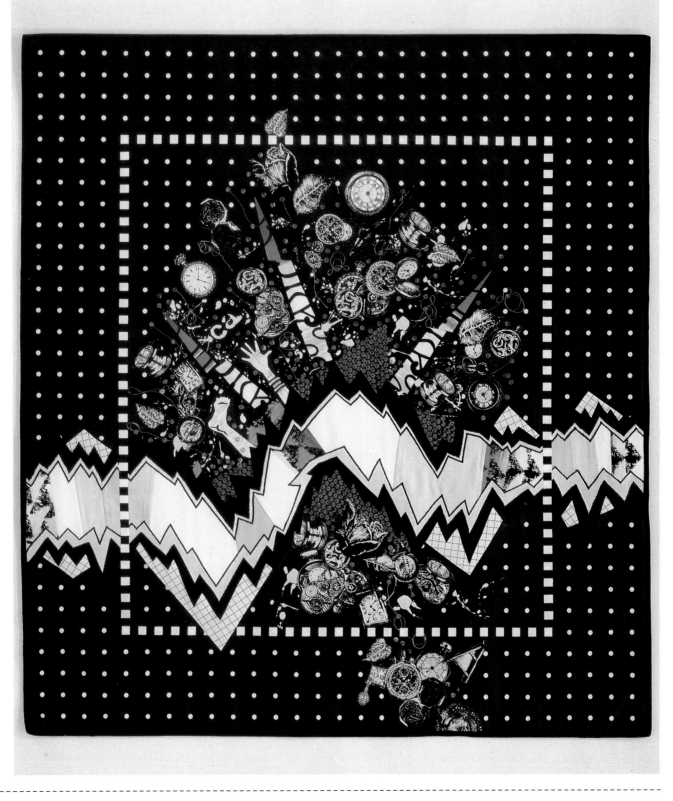

**ADRENALIN**

Deanna Davis (Piedmont, California); 1990; 37 x 47 inches; cottons, cotton blends, laminated paper, fabric paint, metallic thread, and sequins; photo by Sharon Risedorph

I designed this quilt to portray the heart-stopping wrench of the Loma-Prieta Earthquake of 1990. The grids and polka-dot ground symbolize the disintegration of structured lives. My acute adrenaline surge was so clearly expressed to me that the quilt was very painful to complete. Quick techniques were used because my hands became clammy and my fingers shook whenever I came near the quilt. I made this as a reminder that we didn't have flashlights, water, food … anything planned for the "Big One." Do we now? You guessed it. My hands sweat, my fingers shake. Ah, me … Denial!